# CUBAN

## National Reconciliation

Task Force on
**Memory, Truth, and Justice**

Cuban National Reconciliation



University Park, DM 353
Miami, Florida 33199
305-348-2894
http://lacc.fiu.edu

http://memoria.fiu.edu
email: memoria@fiu.edu

Translation: Mariela Córdoba
Copy Editor: Ileana Oroza
Cover Design: Francisco Martín, Pedro D. Botta
Graphic Production: Pedro D. Botta


Printed in the United States of America

ISBN 1-879862-22-0

# Contents

# Preface

Approximately three years ago during her stay as visiting professor, Marifeli Pérez-Stable proposed the project on which *Cuban National Reconciliation* is based to the Latin American and Caribbean Center (LACC) at Florida International University (FIU). The objective was to contribute to the process of Cuban national reconciliation by means of a methodology that would combine historical interpretation and comparative analysis. To be honest, our first reaction was somewhat skeptical. In the past twenty years there have been few discussions about Cuba in Miami or anywhere else that did not generate passionate debates and occasional confrontations. Our skepticism mainly pertained to the question she intended to answer in the study. What should be done with a past of human rights violations? This question stems from the controversial assumptions that human rights have been violated in Cuba and that there will come a time when Cubans will have to decide how to answer it, as was the case in many other countries that now have democratic regimes (even if human rights are still being violated in some of them).

The project's objective was ambitious since it was not just a mere academic exercise, but also proposed to involve all those sectors willing to participate. LACC was intrigued by the possibility of establishing an initial agenda for Cuba's national reconciliation through a series of seminars and discussions among historically opposed sectors, for until this project, we had had few opportunities to conduct a conversation with sectors of the Cuban exile community that viewed the Center's activities on Cuba with skepticism.

Financed by the Ford Foundation and the Open Society Institute, the Task Force on Memory, Truth, and Justice is significant because Pérez-Stable and her colleagues succeeded both in debating and proposing possible answers to the difficult question posed, and in making recommendations for Cuba's national reconciliation. The historical account provided by *Cuban National Reconciliation* serves to put in context the question of what to do with a past of human rights violations through an analysis of the experience of other countries. Thus, the report identifies and defines ways in which this question has been approached. Instead of dwelling on the accusations from one side or another, this report analyzes the long list of charges not only against the Cuban government and the violent opposition, but also against the United States.

A review of the experiences in Spain, South Africa, Central America,

Eastern Europe, and the Southern Cone provides an opportunity to understand the complexity of the answers to the central question. It further reveals important lessons that could help Cubans as they attempt to achieve national reconciliation. This report approaches the subject in a distinct manner, combining an academically tested methodology with an overview of how other countries answered the same question. These experiences provide innumerable lessons that are skillfully compiled in *Cuban National Reconciliation.*

Pérez-Stable and her colleagues have successfully established national reconciliation as a long process that can take place only when the old passions that divide people are abandoned. It is a process that depends on democratization and the construction of a state respectful of human rights. At the same time, reconciliation necessarily involves the creation of a tolerant civil society, willing to abide by the rule of law. As the experiences of Spain, South Africa, Central America, Eastern Europe, and the Southern Cone demonstrate, this is a difficult and lengthy process.

Upon reading *Cuban National Reconciliation*, LACC feels pleased and proud of having embraced the task force. We know the report will generate even more debate, but it will also provide a valuable contribution to national reconciliation in Cuba. It is even more gratifying to know that this project has enabled Marifeli Pérez-Stable to become a permanent member of the faculty, joining the ranks of the renowned professors and researchers involved in Cuba-related issues at FIU.

Eduardo A. Gamarra, Ph.D.
Director
Latin American and Caribbean Center
Florida International University
March 2003

# Presentation

*Cuban National Reconciliation* is an unusual report. It looks at a democratic Cuba not yet in sight and raises some issues the country will surely face. What should be done with a legacy of human rights violations once the transition process has begun? The democracies founded since the 1970s have grappled with this question in different ways, and for many, the answer has been to establish a truth commission. Their efforts to come to terms with the past shed light on three central facets of the process: recovering silenced or absent memories, identifying the truth about what happened, and searching for justice. It is, moreover, important to highlight the inconclusive and, in many cases, the painfully insufficient character of democratization and reconciliation in new democracies. Still, democracy–the only political system founded on the rights of citizens to dissent through their own autonomous means without fear of government reprisals–may be expanded, deepened, and reformed. In that sense, the new democracies could not be more different from the dictatorial regimes that preceded them: democracy is nourished by an ethics of means and universal rights, while dictatorships impose absolute ends.

The Task Force on Memory, Truth and Justice deemed it necessary to imagine a democratic Cuba–the only one capable of consolidating national reconciliation–and to reflect on these themes in the hopes of helping those Cubans who will eventually carry out the transition on the island. We make two main recommendations: first, that a dialogue–among all Cubans and with all those interested in Cuba–be held regarding the Cuban civic reunion and, second, that Cubans seek the means to recover our historical memory as a central element of that reunion, which must necessarily be peaceful, inclusive, and democratic.*

Twenty-six members made up the task force: sixteen Cubans from the diaspora and ten persons from other countries. Human rights in Cuba–like in any other country–are not the sole responsibility of Cubans, which is why we included members from other national origins. As a group, the Cubans had not worked together before, and we therefore lacked the needed trust to ease into the discussion of issues as sensitive as the ones we proposed. Furthermore, our personal histories reflected a broad spectrum of experiences, over more than four decades in matters of the revolution, the Cuban government, the opposition, and the exile community. Even though some non-Cuban members had engaged in Cuba-related activities, most had not, and this task force was their first immersion in the subject. Their knowledge and experience regarding human rights, democratic transitions, and the processes of memory, truth, and justice proved invaluable to our work; they also showed an extraordinary good will towards Cuba and Cubans. Above all, they helped us look at Cuba in the light of other experiences, a perspective that–perhaps because of our particular insular nature–we Cubans do not always seek. We hope their prestige and credentials will serve as a bridge to people from other countries who might be interested in looking ahead to Cuban national reconciliation. From the beginning, what motivated all of us was an unflinching commitment to a democratic Cuba, to the eradication of political violence among Cubans, and to a belief in the need to recover Cuban historical memory. In the end, we developed the necessary trust in one another to issue *Cuban National Reconciliation.*

The task force decided not to broach two issues that commonly arise when discussing Cuba: the U.S. embargo and the properties confiscated by the revolutionary government. We did not join the fray on the embargo because we did not have consensus among us on the subject. Neither did we deal with property-related issues: our charge was to deal only with those issues related to the physical damages inflicted upon human beings by political violence.

No doubt, it would have been preferable to conduct the work of the Task Force on Memory, Truth, and Justice in Cuba and with the participation of Cubans from the island. Our objectives–a democratic Cuba, non-violence, and the restoration of memory–were not and are not those of the Cuban government. *Cuban National Reconciliation* is nothing more than an embrace of civic life and an invitation to dialogue–its essence being a respectful discussion among people and groups with different points of view–as the only weapon. Even though all kinds of barriers have been removed, maintaining communication with the island is still not easy, especially with those Cubans who have publicly broken from official Cuba and are risking their lives in the peaceful struggle for a better future. Even more difficult is holding face-to-face meetings between these Cubans on the island and those of us in the diaspora who share their ideals. Neither do circumstances facilitate an exchange with those individuals of professional and personal integrity who work within official Cuba today but who will surely be agents of change in the transition. The signatories of this report emphasize that Cuba's future depends mainly on Cubans living on the island: those who for years have publicly expressed their conviction that the nation can and should belong to all, the millions who from the privacy of their homes desire that this should happen sooner rather than later, and those who within or in the periphery of official Cuba seek changes that could eventually contribute to a democratic transition.

The Task Force on Memory, Truth, and Justice did what was possible: to bring together a group of 26 persons committed to the production of this report.** Metaphorically speaking, it could be said Cuba has 15 provinces, not 14: the fifteenth is the diaspora in the United States and other countries, with its headquarters in Miami. Cubans abroad are also part of Cuba and, as such, we have both the right and the duty to express ourselves regarding any Cuban issue. Although the prerogative on making decisions on Cuba's future belongs to Cubans on the island, we can make a decisive contribution to that prospective national reunion right now: reconciliation among Cubans in the diaspora. We hope the discussion of *Cuban National Reconciliation* in the diaspora takes place in a spirit of true dialogue that is indispensable for the eventual reunion of all Cubans. In recent years, Cubans abroad have taken steps towards making our arena of public discourse more tolerant and open, but we still have work to do, and we will do it.

Writing *Cuban National Reconciliation* was a complex task in view of the ideas that were developed and the many points of view to be considered. The report resulted from three meetings and constant communication among the task force, as well as endless consultations with Cubans from the diaspora and the island. The task force met in Cuernavaca (June 2001), Cancún (April 2002), and Morelos (January 2003). In October 2001 and February 2002, we met with some 25 Cubans in Miami to discuss issues of historical memory and national reconciliation. These meetings unveiled an optimistic microcosm of dialogue and reconciliation. We will go on advancing along that course in the diaspora. We also procured opinions on the draft report from Cubans on the island; in the text, we quote those who replied. Our web page–http://memoria.fiu.edu–is an open portal that will incorporate different views on memory, truth, and justice, including the full comments we received from Cuba and those we may receive once the report circulates. The web page will also contain documents, publications, and links related to Cuban national reconciliation, as well as this report and the original Spanish version.

What did the task force achieve after two years of reflection and discussion? We initiated this process well aware of the historical polarization that characterizes Cuban politics and convinced we could no longer put off creating an *extremo centro* ("extreme center")–not to eliminate the poles of the political spectrum but to create a space for those of us who do not line up with either extreme. Only a Cuban public space inclusive of a wide, strong, and rooted center can harbor and nourish the pluralism imperative for a civic and democratic life among all Cubans. We offer readers an interpretation of Cuba's historical context looking forward to a reconciliation through remembering, while bringing together antagonists, past and present. At the same time, the report does not gloss over the hard truths about the human costs extracted by the revolutionary government, the armed opposition, and the U.S. government in defending their respective ends at all costs. After two years of work, we raise more firmly than ever the bulwarks of dialogue and memory on the road to a democratic Cuba.

*Cuban National Reconciliation* reflects the consensus of the Task Force on Memory, Truth and Justice. Not every member agrees with every phrase of the text, but–with the exception of what has been indicated in the individual comments–everyone agrees with the report's general content and tone, and supports its main recommendations. All signatories do so as individuals; institutional affiliations and mentions of national origins are only for identification purposes. We hope this report stimulates dialogue on recovering memories, establishing the truth, and searching for justice, all looking forward to a civic reunion in Cuba and among all Cubans.

Marifeli Pérez-Stable
Coordinator
Task Force on Memory, Truth, and Justice
March 2003

*Throughout this report the phrase "among all Cubans" includes both Cubans residing on the island and those who reside abroad.

**Members were selected by the steering committee: Marifeli Pérez-Stable, Jorge I. Domínguez and Pedro A. Freyre.

# Members of the Task Force on Memory, Truth, and Justice

**Steering Committee**
Marifeli Pérez-Stable
Jorge I. Domínguez
Pedro A. Freyre

Roberto Álvarez*
Paloma Aguilar Fernández*
Juan Antonio Blanco Gil*
Siro del Castillo*
Elisa Vilano Chovel
María Domínguez
Joseph T. Eldridge*
Mark Falcoff*
Damián Fernández
Lino B. Fernández
Carlos García-Vélez
Fernando González Rey*
Carl-Johan Groth
Carlos Alberto Montaner*
Juan Ernesto Méndez
Eusebio Mujal-León
Olga Nazario
Ronalth Ochaeta
Enrique Patterson
Pedro Pérez Castro*
Patricia Tappatá de Valdez
José Miguel Vivanco
Cristina Warren

*Additional or dissenting comment

# Acknowledgements

A project like the publication of *Cuban National* Reconciliation could not be completed without incurring many debts of gratitude. The list should start with the other 25 members of the task force. When we started, we barely knew one another, but in the end we produced a document that represents us all. Task force members of various national origins supported the Cubans with their intelligence, moderation, patience, and kindness; the mixture of nationalities turned out to be extremely beneficial. Jorge I. Domínguez and Pedro A. Freyre agreed to join me in the steering committee that guided the group's work. Their analytical and organizational skills proved pivotal in its planning and development. I am indebted to Damián Fernández, Lino Fernández, and Olga Nazario for having pressed on me the need to establish links in Miami beyond the task force. Multiple conversations with Orlando Gutiérrez helped me gain a deeper understanding of the exile community.

José Zalaquett–a renowned human rights defense attorney, former president of Amnesty International, and member of Chile's National Commission on Truth and Reconciliation, as well as of the round table convened after Pinochet's arrest in London–came to Miami twice. In February 2001, he met with the steering committee to help us develop and plan our work. A year later he returned to give a talk about the Chilean transition to task force members and other Cubans. Priscilla Hayner and Louis Bickford of the International Center for Transitional Justice in New York helped us define parameters and topics for the report; in addition, Priscilla participated in two of our meetings and made a significant contribution to the section on the experiences of other countries with their transitions. Ana María Salazar performed the difficult task of chairing the three meetings–Cuernavaca (June 2001), Cancún (April 2002), and Morelos (January 2003)–with efficiency, distinction, and courtesy. In Cancún, Tina Rosenberg provided us with an enlightening account of transitions in Eastern Europe. In Morelos, Irena Grudzinska Gross from the Ford Foundation suggested key refinements that greatly improved the report's section on Eastern Europe. Students from the *Instituto Tecnológico Autónomo de México*–Claudia Cárdenas and Julia Denegre–took notes in Cuernavaca; Rocío González of the *Universidad Nacional Autónoma de México*, and Edme Pernia of FIU took notes in Cancún. Mariela Córdoba translated the text; Ileana Oroza copyedited it skillfully.

We received great assistance from FIU. Eduardo Gamarra, director of the Latin American and Caribbean Center, welcomed the project and gave me all his support. Julissa Castellanos–associate director of LACC and an exceptional professional–coordinated the project's administration. Vivian Díaz, Jenny García, and Lourdes Guerra carefully coordinated the logistics of the meetings. Other persons from LACC involved in the project who were equally capable and thoughtful include: Wens Alaniz, Angela Bonilla, Pedro Botta, Roberto Espinoza, and Raquel Jurado. Alma DeRojas provided constant support in research and the endless tasks related to the report's production.

The Ford Foundation and the Open Society Institute (OSI) granted FIU the funds that made *Cuban National Reconciliation* possible. Cristina Eguizábal from the Ford Foundation was an exceptional interlocutor; at OSI, Aryeh Neier and George Vickers endorsed our request for support. Ramón Daubon from the Caribbean Environment and Development Institute–also funded by the Ford Foundation–awarded us a grant for the meeting in Morelos.

Thanks to all for your cooperation and assistance.

Marifeli Pérez-Stable

# Acronyms*

| | |
|---|---|
| ACP | Africa, Caribbean, Pacific |
| ANC | African National Congress |
| ARENA | Nationalist Republican Alliance (El Salvador) |
| CANF | Cuban American National Foundation |
| CCPDH | Cuban Committee for Human Rights |
| CEA | Center for the Study of the Americas |
| CEH | Historical Clarification Commission (Guatemala) |
| CEJIL | Center for Justice and International Law (Washington, D.C.) |
| CELS | Center of Legal and Social Studies (Argentina) |
| CIA | Central Intelligence Agency |
| CID | Independent and Democratic Cuba |
| CLADEHLT | Latin American Commission for the Rights and Freedoms of the Workers and Peoples |
| CNI | National Information Center (Chile) |
| CONADEP | The National Commission on the Disappeared (Argentina) |
| DINA | Directorate of National Intelligence (Chile) |
| ENEC | Cuban National Ecclesiastical Conference |
| ETA | Euskadi ta Askatasuna |
| EU | European Union |
| FACE | Facts About Cuban Exiles |
| FAR | Armed Revolutionary Forces |
| FIU | Florida International University |
| FMLN | Farabundo Martí National Liberation Front |
| FOCAL | Canadian Foundation for the Americas |
| FOIA | Freedom of Information Act |
| GDR | German Democratic Republic |
| IACHR | Inter-American Commission on Human Rights |
| IDASA | Institute for Democracy in South Africa |
| IDB | Inter-American Development Bank |
| ILANUD | The United Nations Latin American Institute for the Prevention of Crime and the Treatment of Offenders |
| INRA | National Institute for Agrarian Reform |
| ISRI | Superior Institute of International Relations |
| LACC | Latin American and Caribbean Center |
| MROM | Reflection Roundtable of the Moderate Opposition |
| NGO | Non-governmental Organization |

| | |
|---|---|
| OAS | Organization of American States |
| OIT | International Labor Organization |
| OSI | Open Society Institute |
| PAC | Civil Defense Patrol (Guatemala) |
| PCC | Communist Party of Cuba |
| PSP | Popular Socialist Party |
| PUND | Party of National Democratic Unity |
| REMHI | Recovery of the Historical Memory Project |
| SELADEH | Latin American Secretariat of Human Rights |
| SERPAJ | Peace and Justice Service (Uruguay) |
| UMAP | Military Unit to Aid Production |
| UN | United Nations |
| UNED | National Distance Education University (Spain) |
| UNITA | National Union for the Total Independence of Angola |
| URNG | Guatemalan National Revolutionary Union |

*Most acronyms are given in their Spanish-language form.

# CUBAN
## National Reconciliation

# Introduction and Executive Summary

A democratic Cuba is not yet in the offing. Even so, *Cuban National Reconciliation* looks in that direction because only through democracy will the diversity and pluralism within the Cuban nation find their proper course. At the beginning of the 21st century, democracy is the only political system capable of protecting civic life. A civic, democratic, and inclusive reunion–in Cuba and among all Cubans–would be the foundation for national reconciliation. Even though full reconciliation is not easily accomplished, we strive to attain it, at least to the level necessary to make democratic life possible among all Cubans. Even if conditions favoring a democratic transition have not yet emerged, this report considers that a serious and judicious dialogue about it is salutary and indispensable–first, among all Cubans on the island and abroad, and also with and for all those anywhere who may be interested in Cuba's future. That is our main recommendation, and it is in the spirit of reconciliation that we present this report.

*Cuban National Reconciliation* looks forward to the establishment of a truly democratic Cuba, since only the rule of law is capable of guaranteeing the necessary degree of reconciliation for Cubans to live in peace. This report does not propose one or another specific political program. Its platform is very broad–an inalienable commitment to human rights–and its sole demand is that this commitment be assumed without hesitation. By dialogue we understand a respectful discussion among people and groups with different points of view who–willing to listen to one another–seek an agreement or, at least, a partial bridging of their differences. What *Cuban National Reconciliation* calls for is nothing more than an ethics of means–respect for human rights–that guarantees the only outcome that admits no compromise: a civic and democratic life for all Cubans.

Well before the revolution, Cuban politics tended towards polarization: Cubans confronted one another over causes they considered just and, more often than not, valued these causes more than the means used in their pursuit. Though broad and plural, the political spectrum before 1959 did not nurture a true culture of dialogue among opponents nor a strong commitment to democratic institutions. Politics, understood as give-and-take, slowly lost credibility, and violence gained ascendance as a means to defeat enemies. As just means receded, the Cuban arena for public discourse narrowed. With the coup d'état on March 10, 1952, Fulgencio Batista undermined constitutional rule, installed a repressive regime, and violated human rights. Efforts to negotiate a return to democracy failed; armed struggle decided the fall of the dictatorship. In the view of almost all Cubans, the triumph of the revolution on New Year's Day 1959 offered the nation an extraordinary opportunity for a new national foundation.

Though at first the revolution opened up the public arena, it soon closed off access to anyone who did not second the views on social justice and independence from the United States espoused by the top leadership. Radicalization entailed the elimination of capitalism, the suppression of independent institutions to settle political differences, and a turn towards the Soviet Union. When a cause values absolute partisan ends over just means, it ceases to be a just cause no matter how laudable, and even if it enjoys majority support, as was the case in Cuba at the beginning of the revolution. The great majority of those who opposed the revolution's radicalization believed that restrictions on freedom, total state control over the economy, and an alliance with communism debased Cuban aspirations for democracy and freedom. The demand for iron-clad loyalty to the country, the revolution, and the maximum leader provoked the political polarization. Though the cold war aggravated it, the roots of the polarization were Cuban. Over the ensuing decades, the Cuban government has excluded more and more Cubans from the public arena by suppressing the rich pluralism in Cuban society and even within its own ranks.

*Cuban National Reconciliation* rejects all platforms based on absolute partisan ends, for they necessarily entail the exclusion of those who do not share them. By contrast, this report proposes Cubans adopt an ethics of means: an inalienable commitment to human rights based on inclusion and respect for and among all citizens. Only a state founded on the rights of citizens to dissent–by their own means and without fear of reprisals–will be capable of achieving peace among Cubans. As long as Cuba's political spectrum remains closed to pluralism and dialogue, it will not deserve to be called democratic. No one, and no group, has a prerogative to reason: every Cuban has the right to express himself or herself and, also, the duty to listen. The first bastion of democracy is a political culture broadly rooted on a citizen ethics that is respectful of rights and duties. This report seeks a dialogue aimed at strengthening a new culture of inclusion and responsibility among all Cubans.

*Cuban National Reconciliation* is focused on a question Cubans will almost certainly have to face upon embarking on a transition to democracy: what should be done with a past of human rights violations? The recovery of historical memory, the arrival at truths regarding what actually happened in Cuba, and the search for justice are not easy subjects. Precisely because Cuban politics have been polarized, the tendency has been to justify what happened on the basis of the causes upheld by each of the sides. The experiences of new democracies since the 1970s underscore the importance of reconsidering the history that, in each case, led to polarization–not to belittle ideals or renew confrontations–but to gain a new understanding of how inviolable just means should be for civic life.

Even though this report offers some broad explanations for Cuba's polarization, in no way whatsoever do we pretend to have covered all its complexity nor do we claim our reading of the events to be the only possible one. We do, however, insist that the logical conclusion of the Cuban historical experience is that civic life should be the only inviolable end. We offer these explanations–not to reenact old differences or declare a new round of winners and losers–but in the hope of encouraging a dialogue that moves Cubans closer to a political culture based on citizen rights and duties. These explanations should in no way be construed as justifications for human rights violations. We wholly and unequivocally condemn those perpetrated by the Cuban government as well as the abuses incurred by the armed opposition.[1] Yet, since governments should be the main guarantors of human rights, their responsibility is incomparably higher when such rights are breached; moreover, governments always have at their disposal more numerous and powerful resources to impose their will. In the future, a new discourse of inclusion and national reconciliation will thus have to be crafted by those in power, acknowledging the state's responsibility in deepening and maintaining the political polarization among Cubans after 1959.

In order to frame the discussion on violations and abuses, *Cuban National Reconciliation* lists the principal international agreements on human rights and humanitarian law and proposes them to Cubans as a counterweight to absolute partisan ends. Today, more than ever, they represent broadly accepted standards for political coexistence, the treatment of prisoners, and the conduct of war. Whether or not the Cuban state or its current government has signed them, we consider them ethical and legal guideposts that bolster Cuba's national interest because they facilitate a civic and democratic life among all Cubans. The report provides a list of allegations, facts, and questions regarding government violations and abuses perpetrated by the violent opposition that, one way or another, need to be investigated so that the truth of what happened in Cuba is credibly established among Cubans everywhere; it is, however, a partial list, pending what future investigations may reveal. The U.S. government's participation in violent acts against the Cuban government is also discussed. We also thought it useful to delimit two periods since 1959 during which violations were committed: the 1960s, when the government faced an extensive armed resistance and–according to what we currently know–the worst and most widespread violations happened, and the decades since 1970, when a nonviolent opposition emerged and repression has tended to rely on intimidation, harassment, arbitrariness, and imprisonment. Our second recommendation is that, by whichever way, Cubans should strive to recover their historical memory.

*Cuban National Reconciliation* opens with an overview of the broad international consensus on democracy and human rights, forged more energetically after the cold war, though the Universal Declaration of Human Rights (1948) had long established the basic guidelines on the matter. After 1989, two realities marked Cuba's international relations: the government's opposition to the international consensus on human rights and a near universal opposition to the U.S. embargo. The constitution and the criminal code in effect in Cuba are extraordinarily restrictive of individual freedoms, emphatically prohibitive of all peaceful opposition, and supportive of a far-reaching policy of silencing and intimidating the citizenry. Thus, the rights of all citizens–not just the rights of opponents and human rights activists–are disregarded on a daily basis by the Cuban government.[2] As a result, the United Nations Commission on Human Rights has approved resolutions condemning the human rights situation in Cuba, and the European Union has conditioned economic cooperation to the Cuban government abiding by the principal international agreements on this issue. Especially after the cold war, the character of the Cuban political system figures prominently in its international relations–a consequence of the island's geographical location and its status as a weak power.

The report then sheds some light on the Cuban historical context with the purpose of highlighting the different ways in which polarization took place and how the revolution drastically aggravated it. Though the cold war deepened the Cuban conflict, the United States and the Soviet Union were not its main actors. We underline the fact the revolutionary government had a genuine Cuban opposition on the island and, thus, national reconciliation also implies a recognition of this opposition's own personality and political program, the coincidences and shared ideals with the United States given the cold war context notwithstanding. Relations between the Cuban government and the organized opposition throughout the decades are also sketched, drawing hope from the affirmation of nonviolence by most opponents of official Cuba, on the island and in the diaspora. It is also worth noting that exiles–after decades of seeing themselves as the main opposition to the Cuban government–today freely admit that opponents and human rights activists on the island should play the leading roles.

*Cuban National Reconciliation* subsequently outlines the experiences of other countries–new democracies from the 1970s onward–regarding historical memory and the search for truth and justice: Argentina, Chile, and Uruguay in the Southern Cone; El Salvador and Guatemala in Central America; Czechoslovakia, Albania, Bulgaria, Romania, Poland, Hungary, and Germany in Eastern Europe; Spain; and South Africa. These cases share with Cuba a fundamental characteristic: human rights were violated because a logic of absolute partisan ends took over politics and allowed the use of violence to exclude those who dissented. In this regard, the ideological profile of the different regimes and the popular support some of them had are not the gist of our considerations. These experiences equally underline the broad array of factors that influence transitions and the answers given to the question of what should be done with a legacy of human rights violations.

The following section, "The Issue of Human Rights in Cuba: Past and Present," focuses on two realities. First, the international community readily acknowledges current violations of civil and political rights by the Cuban government. In fact, a large number of countries demand that these rights be respected as a condition to fully normalize their relations with Havana. Second, the history of human rights violations–especially, but not exclusively, in the 1960s–has not been equally acknowledged and, therefore, needs full clarification as a prelude to a democratic Cuba. That future Cuba–responsive to the demands from Cuban civil society, to the experiences of other countries, and to international norms regarding humanitarian law–will have to determine if war crimes and crimes against humanity were committed after 1959, and, if so, to identify those responsible for such crimes which do not have a statute of limitations. A democratic Cuba should also follow the example of most democracies by abolishing the death penalty.

We conclude with an outline of four key elements in the long process of Cuban national reconciliation:

- Reconciliation of every Cuban with himself or herself.

- Family reconciliation, which is the one most advanced to date.

- Reconciliation in the diaspora, which is the one within reach and should not be postponed.

- Political reconciliation–sustained by a civic awareness of citizenship rights and duties–which will only be fully attained under the protection of a state respectful of the citizenry's right to dissent through autonomous means without fears of reprisals.

## International Consensus on Democracy and Human Rights

Although the global character of human rights was proclaimed by the Universal Declaration of Human Rights, a broader consensus on its implementation could not be reached until after the cold war. For decades it was relatively easy to condition the issue to the conflict between the United States and the Soviet Union: on the one hand, Western democracies respected civil and political rights while providing an unevenly matched array of social and economic rights; on the other, in the U.S.S.R. and Eastern Europe–the so-called people's democracies–the social safety net was extended more equally, while individual liberties were banned or severed.[3] During the 1970s, this division began to be questioned by, among others, the Helsinki Final Act, which established the interdependence among political, civil, economic, social, and cultural rights. Furthermore, the Helsinki agreement granted legitimacy to the idea that human rights concerned the international community, not just individual countries. Subsequently, men and women from all nations rose up against violations in other countries, though their protest did not necessarily imply support for regime change in those places. It was then that the international human rights movement took off.

At the beginning of the 21st century, cold war relativism regarding human rights has little resonance, and not only because that war is over. The international consensus on human rights has arisen mainly due to the new democracies that emerged beginning in the 1970s. Under the rule of law, no political objective–no matter how edifying it may be proclaimed to be–justifies the violation of life, of people's personal safety, of the right against arbitrary arrest, and the right to due process, nor of freedoms of speech, association, and conscience. Though imperfect and incomplete, democracy leads to civil and political freedoms, and provides the means for self-determination according to the citizenry's (changing) will. Its essence is a demanding consensus on the respect for human rights that needs, allows, and encourages differences while offering an institutional framework to settle them. At a minimum, democracy is a political system that guarantees the rights of a peaceful opposition and offers it the possibility of gaining power in free elections. The work to establish these facts irrefutably has been long and arduous, and it is those who lived under dictatorships until recently who best understand them.

Nevertheless, the Cuban government continues adhering to a relativist conception of human rights. Its constitution and criminal code categorically prohibit peaceful opposition and endorse wide-ranging policies aimed at silencing and intimidating the citizenry, which constitutes a violation of everyone's civil and political rights. In fact, the Cuban government subordinates citizen rights to what the ruling elites and a sector of the population understand as the common good and the national interest. Cuba was one of the first countries to proclaim the Universal Declaration, and the Cuban state must respect it entirely. In the Western Hemisphere, the American Declaration of the Rights and Duties of Man (1948) and the American Convention on Human Rights (1968) have served, since then, as a beacon in the difficult path towards democracy. The Cuban state signed the first, but not the second.[4] Moreover, the Inter-American Democratic Charter–approved by the Organization of American States (OAS) in 2001–reaffirms representative democracy as essential for the stability, peace, and development of the hemisphere's people. Neither the present nor any future government in Havana will be able to pursue full hemispheric insertion without endorsing the basic principles on human rights and democracy included in these documents.

## Cuba's International Context in the 1990s and Early 21st Century

Two facts have marked Cuba's international relations in the post-cold war period: its government's opposition to the broad international consensus on human rights, and the ample dissent regarding the U.S. embargo.[5] In 1992, the United Nations General Assembly approved two resolutions that expressed the wishes of most members: that the United States lift the embargo, and that Cuba carry out economic and political reforms. At the beginning of the new century, neither has materialized.

While the United States reinforced the embargo through the Torricelli (1992) and the Helms-Burton (1996) acts, the European Union (EU), Canada, and Latin America set the basis for a policy of so-called constructive engagement and repudiated the U.S. laws. Still, an easing of tensions between the United States and Cuba has taken place on two fronts. In 1994, Havana and Washington signed a new migratory agreement that has entailed regular contact to examine its implementation.[6] Similarly, the United States and Cuba have generally encouraged and supported cultural and academic exchanges. Since 1996, the EU has annually ratified a common position regarding Cuba along the lines normally demanded from its trading partners: compliance with the international agreements and norms on human rights as a prior step to economic cooperation (humanitarian cooperation is not conditioned). Though differently, both the United States and the European Union condition their relations with Havana to the Cuban government's implementation of domestic changes. While human rights violations by any government (e.g. China, Vietnam, or Saudi Arabia) are always deplorable, the situation for Cuba has been different. Especially in the post-cold war period, the character of the Cuban political system weighs heavily on its international relations–politics and geography have thus determined it. It is undoubtedly unfortunate that different standards are applied to similar situations regarding human rights, particularly when these double standards undermine the credibility of the claim to their universality. Nevertheless, the unequal treatment given to violators has not become an obstacle to the ever stronger consolidation of the international consensus regarding democracy and human rights.

After the fall of the Berlin Wall and, especially, after the downfall of the Soviet Union, Cuba lost its main allies and was forced to restructure its relationship with the world. When its economy collapsed, the government decreed a certain liberalization regarding foreign investment, self-employment, independent work, agricultural cooperatives, and the U.S. dollar as legal tender. These measures reduced the state's role, partially loosened the official ties that determined people's livelihood until 1990, and reactivated the economy slightly. However, there have been no noteworthy political changes regarding the monopoly of the Communist Party nor, in general, regarding human rights. Still, the government has not been able to exercise the same control on society, as evidenced by the ascendant strength and geographical expansion of civil society activities as counterparts to official ones.[7]

The policy of constructive engagement adopted by the European Union, Canada, and Latin America was aimed at encouraging changes in Cuba. Canada took great pains to nudge Cuba in that direction when it offered economic cooperation, humanitarian assistance, and development aid without political conditions, as well as efforts to help the island's hemispheric reinsertion. Though modest, the economic reforms that were implemented suggested the possibility of a new round to consolidate the economy, e.g., the legalization of small- and medium-sized private business and the easing of regulations regarding foreign investment. Spain, Portugal, and Latin America also made considerable efforts to encourage changes in the island. Spain's determination to facilitate Cuba's soft landing in the new international context was particularly notable. During the first Iberoamerican summits, Mexico, Colombia, and Spain pressed Castro on the importance that he be the one to lead the reform process. Iberoamerican countries also backed the Cuban government concerning the embargo. The following quote from the final declaration at Cartagena de Indias, Colombia (1994) best expresses the condemnation of the embargo regularly issued at these summits:

> We recommend the elimination, in accordance with the principles of international law and with U.N. resolutions, of unilateral coercive economic and commercial measures that may affect the free development of international commerce and harm the living conditions of Latin American peoples.

At the same time, the summits have also been unequivocal regarding democracy. The summit in Chile (1996) issued a final declaration, signed by Fidel Castro, stating the following:

> We reassert our commitment to democracy, the rule of law, and political pluralism. There exists in Iberoamerica the conviction

> that the separation of powers, their mutual control, proper representation and participation of majorities and minorities, freedom of speech, of association and reunion, full access to information, free, regular, and transparent elections of political leaders, constitute essential elements of democracy.

Through the United Nations, the international community has also expressed its dissatisfaction with the embargo and with the absence of civil and political freedoms in Cuba. Overwhelming majorities at the General Assembly have annually approved a resolution against the policy of isolation implemented by the United States.[8] Since 1991, the Human Rights Commission at Geneva has been passing resolutions condemning the Cuban situation. Only in 1998 was the motion defeated, mainly as an acknowledgement of the government's partial restoration of religious freedom and the release of some 300 prisoners on the occasion of Pope John Paul II's visit to Cuba that year.[9] In 1999, the commission once again issued a resolution condemning Cuba. Not only had Cuba's National Assembly passed an exceptionally draconian law against freedom of expression, but four opponents who had been held in preventive detention without bail since 1997 were tried and convicted.

The 2002 resolution was approved under novel conditions: in 2001, the United States was not reelected as a full commission member and had only observer status. The resolution critical of Cuba–promoted mainly by the Latin American members–obtained the favorable vote of the region's countries represented on the commission, except for Venezuela, which voted against it and Ecuador which abstained.[10] Nevertheless, the wording of the resolution has been the most moderate to date. It reads:

> The commission invites the Government of Cuba, whose efforts to give effect to the social rights of the population despite an adverse international environment are to be recognized, to make efforts to achieve similar progress in respect of human, civil and political rights, in accordance with the provisions of the Universal Declaration of Human Rights and the principles and standards of the rule of law.

Mexico's vote was especially pointed as it was the first time it backed a resolution against Cuba.

By the mid 1990s, the isolation of the Cuban government intended by the United States had been prevented by the policy of constructive engagement and by the effectiveness of Cuba's Ministry of Foreign Relations. Cuba had diplomatic relations with 178 countries and commercial relations with 166, and had increased links with Latin America and the Caribbean. Except for the United States, there was consensus regarding the island's insertion into the international economy. In fact, the world had opened up to Cuba before Pope John Paul II offered his memorable farewell to the island: "May Cuba open itself up to the world, and may the world open itself up to Cuba." However, Cuba's opening to the world has not ensued due to the Cuban government's unwillingness to reciprocate the European Union, Canada, and Latin America in their constructive engagement. On the matter of human rights, it showed little cooperation. Although Cuba allowed the visit of the United Nations High Commissioner for Human Rights in 1994, Havana never acquiesced to that of the special rapporteur appointed by the United Nations (1992-1998) to deal with the human rights situation in Cuba.[11]

In the mid-1990s, the European Union initiated conversations with the Cuban government to reach an economic cooperation agreement and to discuss issues related to human rights. The European Union's conditions were and are: releasing political prisoners, reforming the criminal code (especially the abolition of the death penalty), and ratifying the International Covenant on Civil and Political Rights. Conversations between the European Union and Havana coincided with the request to the government by Cuban Council–an opposition coalition formed in October 1995–to hold a meeting at the end of February 1996. Some thought the request would be granted in light of the EU talks, but it was not. Worse still, Cuban air force MIG fighter jets shot down two civilian planes belonging to Brothers to the Rescue; four men were killed. At the time, the Helms-Burton bill was making little progress in the U.S. Congress, partly due to President William J. Clinton's veto threat; after the planes were downed, the toughest version of Helms-Burton was quickly enacted into law.[12] A political dialogue between the European Union and Cuba is still pending; for it to be productive, the Cuban government must agree to discuss matters of human rights, a negotiation it has thus far refused.

Neither constructive engagement by Europe, Canada, and Latin America nor confrontation by the United States have managed to trigger a process of real change toward the democratization of Cuba. In any case, the political climate in the United States at the beginning of 2003 might lead to easing travel restrictions to the island and allowing the U.S. financing of Cuban food purchases.[13] Without advocating sanctions, the European Union, Canada, and Latin America are placing more emphasis on human rights in their dealings with Cuba. Though Canada continues to be an important trade partner and to provide technical and humanitarian assistance, Ottawa adjusted its previous policy in 1999. Since then, it has conditioned Cuba's integration into the Inter-American System to a clear process of political and economic reform. In 2002, at a meeting of the European Union and the African, Caribbean, and Pacific group (ACP), to which Cuba belongs, the European Union reiterated its position that Cuba's access to economic development funds should be restricted as long as the Cuban government did not accept a political dialogue on human rights. Even before Vicente Fox's victory in the 2002 elections, relations between Mexico and Cuba were growing tense as a result of the influence that ongoing political changes in Mexico were exerting on that country's foreign policy. In 1999, President Ernesto Zedillo delivered a strong, pro-democracy speech at the Iberoamerican summit in Havana and asked then Mexican foreign minister, Rosario Green, to meet with a prominent human rights activist, Elizardo Sánchez Santacruz.

While in Havana for the summit, King Juan Carlos I of Spain uttered a memorable phrase that complemented the pope's: "Let Cuba open itself to Cuba." Together, these simple phrases mark guidelines for the island's full integration into the world of the early 21st century. Only if the Cuban government moves toward guaranteeing civil and political rights will Cuba's international situation begin to normalize. For cultural and historical reasons, Cuba is part of Latin America, and today democracy–its painful inadequacies notwithstanding–is the marker of Latin America. In contrast, the Cuban government refuses to admit either the growing pluralism in Cuban society or the pluralism from within its own ranks. This obstinacy is the main reason why today the world is asking so insistently: "Why doesn't Cuba change?"

More significant still is that this question has been and is being asked from the heart of Cuba. Sensible ideas to restructure the economy and to allow for some political flexibility have come up repeatedly from within the government's ranks, but the top leadership has ignored them.[14] When the same ideas have been put forward by the organized opposition, the government has responded with force and harassment. When Félix Bonne Carcassés, René Gómez Manzano, Vladimiro Roca

Antúnez, and Marta Beatriz Roque Cabello submitted to the authorities a document called *La Patria es de Todos* ('The Homeland Belongs to Us All'), critical of the lack of freedoms, the country's economic policy, and the misrepresentation of history, the official answer was to imprison them.[15] When Oswaldo Payá Sardiñas and the promoters of the Varela Project[16]–a civic action based on constitutional clauses that grant citizens the right to propose legal changes and ask for a referendum to decide upon them–managed 11,020 signatures and duly submitted them to the National Assembly in May 2002, they received no official answer. The government, however, responded indirectly with a counter petition declaring socialism irrevocable and amending the constitution to so reflect it. For now, official Cuba has closed most doors to the other Cuba: that which, from within the elite or from the homes of ordinary Cubans, proposes and hopes for profound changes.

At the beginning of the 21st century, the strategic coincidence between the United States and its allies on a democratic future for Cuba has been gaining prominence. In any case, that future depends mainly on the efforts made in Cuba and by all Cubans, not on one country's foreign policy or another's. During his extraordinary visit to Cuba in May 2002, former President James E. Carter–while condemning the embargo–also said: "I should add that these restraints are not the source of Cuba's economic problems." Carter spoke clearly about the limitations on the freedom of expression and of association that impede the actions of a peaceful opposition; he also praised the Varela Project for seeking legal change via constitutional channels. Democracy, Carter implied, promotes national sovereignty: "When Cubans exercise this freedom to change laws peacefully by a direct vote, the world will see that Cubans, and not foreigners, will decide the future of this country."

## The Cuban Historical Context

*My two children died fighting for Cuba's freedom: one with one idea, the other with another.*

Marcelina Chacón
Cumanayagua, Escambray Mountains, 1963[17]

Though on occasions, before 1959, some political groups subscribed to nonviolence to obtain their objectives, this is the first time in Cuban history the vast majority of the organized opposition to a dictatorship rejects violence. The current opposition struggle is being waged for human rights and from a position respectful of these rights; its political and civic activity is rooted in an ethic of just means. Significant in and of itself, this fact is even more so when placed in the context of a political culture that, since the independence wars of the 19th century, has valued the use of violence–often indiscriminately–as a means to settle political conflicts. Though the present polarization is unprecedented, Cuban politics was becoming polarized well before January 1, 1959. From the 1920s onward, especially after the revolution of 1933 that overthrew Gerardo Machado's regime, intransigence became deeply rooted in Cuban politics: means were often sidestepped in favor of an absolutism that did not admit any consideration other than full attainment of its objectives.[18] Cubans easily defined themselves as victors or losers, adversaries were frequently considered enemies, and those who conciliated or negotiated were often deemed traitors. Although the political spectrum was broad and pluralistic, it did not spawn a culture of dialogue and commitment to democratic institutions. Not surprisingly, violence started gaining more and more legitimacy, to the point of displacing other ways of settling political differences. Following the coup on March 10, 1952, it became impossible to find a negotiated way out of the Batista regime. After 1956, armed struggle became the main front against a regime of corruption, repression, and violation of democratic norms and human rights. The revolutionary victory only worsened the nation's polarization and violence.

The March 10th coup was preceded by twelve years of democratic governments. The Constitution of 1940–strongly democratic, committed to social justice, and of nationalist intent–embodied popular aspirations. Its enactment was the zenith of Cuban conciliation in the 20th century–signed by all political groups and, above all, crafted and agreed upon exclusively by Cubans. Its ratification in Guáimaro–where the Constitution governing the republic in arms during the Ten Years' War (1868-1878) against Spain had been approved–rendered a symbol of a new national foundation. The Platt amendment had been abolished in 1934.[19] The period's most important achievement was respecting civil and political freedoms as never before. Cuba was actually one of the few democracies in Latin America, and Cubans were recognized for their "deep-seated and indestructible democratic idiosyncrasy."[20] Those years, however, are better known for their failings. Corruption was the most galling, not for its novelty, but for the fact that it had been perpetrated by the generation that had ousted Machado in order to change Cuba. Neither did democracy completely displace political violence, witness the so-called action groups which regularly used force to settle disputes at universities, unions, and in other spheres. At the same time, neither congress nor the executive moved to sponsor legislation to fully complement the constitution. Blacks and mulattos, for example, waited in vain for legal guarantees of their equality and for laws that imposed penalties for racial discrimination, as prescribed by the constitution; the absence of such legislation constituted a massive violation of their citizen rights. On the whole, democracy did not consolidate sufficiently to promote solid institutions, an effective political class, and the citizenry's trust. Even so, the restoration of the Constitution of 1940 was the main platform against Batista, universally espoused by the organized opposition including the July 26 Movement and the Rebel Army.

By the 1950s, a deep feeling of uneasiness had seeped through Cuban national culture. Only six decades after independence, Cuba had experienced rather impressive material progress, though not enough to satisfy Cubans' high expectations and, especially, without noticeably redressing two serious social problems: unemployment and the living conditions of the peasantry. Nonetheless, Cuban society had an influential and vibrant middle class–including rising middle sectors among blacks and mulattos. The support that the United States gave Batista until nearly the end of his dictatorship, however, reinforced nationalist sentiments that the revolutionary government would later channel for its own pursuits. After efforts to negotiate a peaceful transition to democracy failed, public opinion slowly embraced the rebels and armed struggle.

Fidel Castro's words in Santiago de Cuba on January 1, 1959, well expressed the national mood at the time:

> This time Cuba is fortunate: the revolution will truly come to power. It will not be as in 1895 when the Americans intervened at the last minute and appropriated our country...It will not be as in 1933 when the people believed the revolution was in the making and Batista...usurped power...It will not be as in 1944 when the masses were exuberant in the belief that they had at last come to power but thieves came to power instead. No thieves, no traitors, no interventionists! This time the revolution is for real!

Throughout the republic, the term 'revolution' signified the hope that one day Cuba would fully realize José Martí's dream of sovereignty, justice, and democracy. As the decades passed, the dream seemed ever farther, even if it continued to figure prominently in the national imagination. At the end of the 1950s, Cuba's political culture–the ideas and passions that underpin politics–leaned toward intolerance. People had lost their patience and demanded the country be led down the right path, once and for all. The overwhelming majority listened to *Comandante* Fidel Castro when he descended from the Sierra Maestra and gave him their trust. "This is a decisive moment in our history: tyranny has been defeated. Our happiness is immense, but we have much yet to do," he said upon his arrival in Havana on January 8, 1959.

## The Radicalization of the Revolution and Its Consequences

The vast majority of Cubans embraced the revolution convinced that their hopes for social justice, national sovereignty, and democracy would finally be realized. The Constitution of 1940 had been the platform of the organized opposition to Batista, which meant a commitment to democracy, good government, and profound socioeconomic reforms. From the outset, however, the basis for a democratic restoration was neglected: the Fundamental Law of February 7, 1959–issued by the Council of Ministers–gave that same council virtually unchecked legislative faculties. Most council members would soon join the opposition or go into exile. Though democrats in spirit, even they, in the early days, saw the revolution as the absolute source of legal rights, to be defended at all costs and for which it was justified to set aside–albeit temporarily–the balance of powers essential for democracy. But there was no turning back. The Fundamental Law facilitated the centralization of political and economic power the revolutionary leaders would push for relentlessly over the ensuing 18 months.

Towards the end of 1960, Cuba was no longer a capitalist country, and the institutions capable of settling political conflict peacefully had disappeared. The anti-Batista opposition had rallied around other principles–the restoration of democracy and an economic transformation that would redress social problems–but, still, the government retained great popular support. Those who backed it had already established such a strong emotional bond with the revolution that *la revolución* became a quasi-mystical symbol whose pull is still felt by some sectors in Cuban society. Defending national sovereignty against the United States, and what was understood as social justice, displaced democracy, and the revolutionary majority at the time never considered the consequences. Throughout 1959 and 1960, the vast majority of those who came to oppose the radicalization of the revolution still saw the need for a profound socioeconomic transformation and a moderate nationalism. The following words are a clear expression of this position:

> We wanted economic growth governed by the idea that it was necessary to place the economy at the service of people. And this would not happen without an economic plan respectful of private property but controlling it; without regulating foreign investment so that it really became useful for our country; without a land reform; without a sound industrialization policy. We wanted social development: agrarian transformations, improvements in standards of living, expansion of public education, and the eradication of all types of discrimination.[21]

Though land reform and the subsequent nationalizations alienated the upper class and large sectors of the middle class, just as relevant–perhaps more so–for the emergence of an organized opposition after 1959 was the way the top leadership monopolized the right to determine what needed to be done. As never before in Cuban history, the revolutionary government assumed a logic of absolute partisan ends that quickly merged the country with the revolution and the revolution with its maximum leader. That merger of country, revolution, and leadership was the banner the government defended and still defends without quarter. Loyalty was and is indivisible: one could not and cannot be loyal to the country without unconditionally being loyal to the other two. In that context, the organized opposition–resuming the fight for the restoration of democracy–resorted to armed rebellion, a recourse normally recognized as valid when other options have disappeared, though under strict humanitarian criteria, such as those listed on pages 56-57.

Between 1960 and 1966, thousands of Cubans–including peasants and other citizens of humble origins, among them not a few veterans of the Rebel Army, the Revolutionary Directorate and the Second Front in Escambray–took up arms against the revolutionary government.[22] On the one hand, the organized opposition responded in consonance with a political culture that almost always valued the force of arms over a nonviolent struggle in confronting a dictatorship. On the other, the revolutionary government reined in all autonomous political activity–as was the case with labor unions and at universities–and took drastic measures against the organized opposition. Under these circumstances, the latter's resort to arms was almost inevitable. Though Escambray was the heart of the resistance, there were some 179 rebel groups across the island; the official discourse labeled them "bandits." At least 3,000 lives were lost in the conflict.[23] The abuses committed by the violent opposition–their character and extent–will have to be determined in the future; a list of facts and questions appears on pages 60-61. During these years, the government faced a greater number of rebels than had fought against Batista. The Revolutionary Armed Forces mobilized some 100,000 militias to combat the rebels, which may have totaled 8,000 at their peak in 1961.[24] The Rebel Army never had more than 2,000 recruits. In the summer of 1958, some 12,000 soldiers took part in a military offensive against the rebels–the only serious assault Batista's army ever mounted in the conflict. During the 1950s, some 2,000 people died as a result of the political violence.[25]

Those who opposed the revolutionary government had many reasons, their ideals of democracy and freedom being the most important. Without doubt, the cold war aggravated the polarization that accompanied the revolution's radicalization: opponents–who rebelled against the nascent dictatorship even more intensely than they had against Batista's–saw the turn towards communism and the Soviet Union as an additional affront to Cuban ideals of independence and sovereignty. They had also been part of the revolutionary coalition that toppled Batista, and now the revolutionary government excluded them. Those Cubans who overlooked the consequences of the radicalization did so neither from communist convictions nor because they favored the Soviet Union: they felt the causes of social justice and nationalism espoused by the revolutionary government more vehemently than those the United States and its allies raised during the cold war. Each side claimed nationalism: supporters of the revolutionary government did so against the United States; opponents, against the Soviet Union. Until 1989, the two sides turned either to Washington or Moscow for support of their respective objectives. Nevertheless, for a majority of Cubans, the revolutionary government's nationalist claim against the United States overshadowed that of the opposition's against the Soviet Union. In the eyes of the international community, the Cuban opposition–which had reasons and legitimacy of its own–was encumbered by its alliance with Washington. Its ties with Moscow did not extract a similar political cost from the Cuban government. Any process of national reconciliation should entail a fair recognition of the organized opposition's own political personality and its Cuban profile.

The consequences of the radicalization are still felt, two of them in particular. First, more than a million Cubans have left the island. In the early 1960s, exiles came mainly from the upper and middle classes: the revolutionary government had confiscated their means of livelihood, limited their professional life to state-appointed tasks, and repudiated their ethical and political values. Between 1960 and 1962, more than 14,000 children and adolescents were sent to the United States on their own, due to their parents' fears the revolutionary government would revoke their parental rights.[26] Subsequent waves of Cubans left their country for political and economic reasons. Between 1965 and 1972, people of more humble origins left, their aspirations for social mobility and freedom having been frustrated by socialism. In 1980, the Mariel exodus was led by young people who did not find in Cuban society the place and opportunities they expected. Mariel and the ensuing waves have been the most representative of Cuban society, including many who supported the government for decades and who in the 1990s–already disenchanted–found it difficult to live in Cuba.[27] Emigration has offered the Cuban government a necessary safety valve for exporting malcontents.

The requirement of an incontestable loyalty to the country, the revolution, and its maximum leader sparked the political polarization. In the heat of the revolutionary victory, this loyalty seemed natural for the majority who felt it was a necessary means for achieving a new Cuba. But as a political platform, it was flawed from the outset, and this is the second consequence of the radicalization process that persists today. The imposition of a trinitarian loyalty splintered the anti-Batista coalition: under its terms, no discrepancy on the direction of the revolution was brooked; consequently, there was no room allowed for the peaceful resolution of the legitimate political differences that arose after 1959. Exile, prison, and executions were the price paid by the opposition. That demand for absolute loyalty also discouraged the formulation of alternative proposals within the revolution and within socialism. In no small measure, the gradual erosion of the revolutionary consensus is due to the iron-clad defense of this trinitarian allegiance. The top leadership never found a way to tap into the rich diversity within the revolutionary elite and in society. As a result, the numbers of exiles and political prisoners grew, and a shroud of political silence covered the country, and a *doble moral* developed–people say one thing in public, while privately believing another. The number of Cubans suffering from an "anthropological lesion"–in the words of Monsignor Pedro Meurice Estiu, archbishop of Santiago de Cuba–has increased: they do not feel in control of their lives nor capable of taking responsibility for changing Cuba. It is a situation made even more dramatic by the fact that the Cuban revolution, in its beginning, genuinely represented the hopes of almost all Cubans.

The outlook today is quite different. If at one moment the revolution stood for the aspirations of the majority, today the government not only has turned its back on the calls for change from a good many citizens, but has also shunned those within its own ranks willing to bring about change. Only a platform of national reconciliation that allows a civic and democratic reunion in Cuba and among all Cubans will overcome the current impasse. Cuba is broken into pieces, and Cubans will not be able to put it together again by reasserting the polarization that led to the country's political ruin. Cubans of goodwill–wherever they live–need to become fully aware of their history and of their inadequate civic ethics. The premises for a lasting civic reunion and a new national foundation are:

- That political differences–desirable and necessary–require democratic institutions to bridge them and guarantees for the opposition to exercise its legitimate functions of peaceful dissent and political challenge at the polls; and

- That no group, sector, or individual has the right to claim to be the sole interpreter or bearer of the national interest.

When human rights become the only and steadfast political platform, Cubans will be able to live in peace.

When civic coexistence is hoisted as an inviolable goal, violence among Cubans will have been forever banished.

Simply said: The homeland belongs to all of us.[28]

## Government and the Organized Opposition After 1959

From the start, the revolutionary government interwove two strands: one inclusive, the other exclusive. In the early 1960s, most Cubans supported the revolution and its ideals. The revolutionary government implemented agrarian and urban reforms that favored the popular classes and served to consolidate their support. It also projected policies that, once enforced, diminished the differences between urban and rural Cuba, and widened access to education and public health.[29] At the same time, confrontation with the United States let loose such unbridled nationalism that the famous cry–*¡Cuba sí, Yankis no!*–burst out of the hearts and minds of millions of Cubans. The revolution served as prelude to the 1960s, as it inserted itself into the national liberation movements in Africa and Asia. Later, it became a symbol for the rebellious youth in the United States, Latin America and Europe who, by the late 1960s, protested *en masse* against the Vietnam war and considered socialism a viable political alternative. In Cuba, an undetermined number of people still support the revolution for what it once was and for the achievements they attribute to it. A greater number still–though unhappy with the official paralysis that has prevailed since the mid-1990s and desirous of reform–cherish the ideals of the 1960s and fear that a radical change of the status quo would undermine social justice and national sovereignty.

The revolution and the government that followed it also imposed an absolute logic of exclusion. At the beginning, it was easy to blame these exclusions on the economic interests affected by the first redistributive measures in favor of the popular classes. Though these measures undoubtedly played a role in the early disaffection of thousands of Cubans, it does not do the historical record justice to understate the importance that ideas, beliefs, and values had in mobilizing the first wave of opponents. The shift that fused the country with the revolution and its maximum leader and sided Cuba with the Soviet Union in the cold war provoked the strongest and deepest of rejections among many Cubans. Communism, after all, not only deprived them of their right to private property, but also of their civil, political, and religious freedoms. A desire to regain these freedoms led thousands of Cubans who were not wealthy, and in fact often came from the most humble origins, to join the opposition. For them, the revolution they had hoped would banish dictatorships once and for all not only turned dictatorial before their very eyes but also aligned Cuba with the communist superpower. At the same time, the Catholic church and many in the laity began confronting the revolutionary government for reasons similar to those offered by the Catholic opposition in Poland and Hungary during the 1950s: communism curtailed religious freedom and proclaimed atheism as the official ideology; religion, thus, became a logical motivator for many opponents. Were not all these turns a betrayal of the Cuban aspirations for freedom and democracy? In the early 1960s, the organized opposition answered with a resounding yes, offered with the same intensity that the majority at the time expressed its support of the revolutionary government.

The fact of the matter was that there were two national projects: the one represented by the radicalized revolution, and the one defended by the organized opposition. The first valued its vision of social justice and national sovereignty against the United States above democracy and freedom; the second rejected the radicalization, especially the idea that loyalty to the country demanded due obedience and unconditional support of the revolutionary government, particularly the maximum leader. The objectives of the organized opposition–genuine and inherently Cuban as they were–disappeared in the fabric of the cold war and the spirit of the New Left in the 1960s. The following observation accurately reflects the dilemma of those who were against the revolution's radical turn:

> I remember a speech by Fidel Castro in 1975, and he was talking about the spirit of the young people at the time, and of the purity of their intentions in early 1959, their desire to build a country, to do right, to put a wedge between what had not worked up to there and what was going forward....I thought to myself: I used to know people like this! The only problem is that they all fought against Mr. Castro.
>
> Part of the frustration that we feel after all these years is that history has been written by the victors. In this case, however, there is a long appendix written mainly by sore losers or people who are trying to dissemble the whole thing, put a spin on it, rationalize it. We can put something important on the record, the force of all those young people, idealistic people who because of

> number one, religious convictions, and number two, because they were evicted from the revolutionary coalition, decided to take up arms against the government.
>
> I don't think that there was a hell of a big chance in April of 1961 for us to be ready to overthrow the government. I am sorry, but I cannot blame the Americans for failure there. It was not your responsibility to liberate Cuba. It was ours. I *can* blame you for getting into a fight and then trying to take over, and then diverting the fight and not allowing for the maturation of the indigenous resistance. Your fault was to get into the fight, to set it up in a way that would accomplish *your* objectives with *our* means, not *our* means with *our* objectives.[30]

That the early opponents of the Cuban government are still portrayed as mere adjuncts to Washington's designs on Cuba remains an open wound. Healing will only come when their ideals and hopes–also quintessentially Cuban–are broadly recognized.[31]

For the United States, the revolution's turn towards the Soviet Union encompassed a grave threat. A communist Cuba, entrenched 90 miles from the United States, could alter the balance between Washington and Moscow, something that almost happened when the Soviet Union placed nuclear missiles on the island in 1962. Shortly after the Bay of Pigs, John F. Kennedy's administration organized Operation Mongoose–a covert plan to destabilize the revolutionary government–which remained in place after the withdrawal of the missiles from Cuba. Between 1961 and 1963, the Central Intelligence Agency (CIA) set up a wide network of covert activities in the United States and abroad, which drew on considerable human and financial resources. Miami was its operational base, and close to 3,000 exiles participated in this campaign. Some sectors of public opinion in Cuba and in the United States consider Operation Mongoose and its offshoots to have been a form of state-sponsored terrorism.

Over decades, the interactions between the Cuban government and the organized opposition changed. In the 1960s, the revolutionary government had the support of a majority of Cubans, and awakened in them unprecedented commitment and hopeful anticipation. For them, it was a decade full of ideals, the purest and most creative years of the revolution when the homeland was truly Cuban. By 1970, however, that revolutionary homeland gave evidence of exhaustion from the constant mobilizations, economic decay, and political impositions that perturbed everyday life. Cuba had been governed as if ordinary Cubans were heroic creatures when, in fact, their aspirations were more mundane. Years later, a high-ranking official characterized the popular mood of the time as one of "resigned support," a marked departure from the euphoria of the early 1960s.[32] Over the decade, tensions and differences arose within the top leadership over an economic policy that disdained what was then known as market socialism, as well as over a foreign policy that actively supported guerrillas, especially in Latin America. Many elites and rank-and-file party members were purged, the most notorious case being the microfaction of 1968, the first great rupture inside the Communist party.[33] Nonetheless, many in Cuba and abroad believed that the revolution was offering a more radical and genuine socialist alternative than the Soviet Union and saw it as a mark of distinction. The ideas and hopes of the New Left dwarfed the precepts of Soviet orthodoxy. In 1968, the Prague Spring–reforms introduced by Czech communists to draw a human face on socialism–awakened enthusiastic interest among important sectors in Cuba, who were sorely disappointed when Fidel Castro supported the Soviet invasion of Czechoslovakia.

But there was another country in the 1960s: that of Cubans who opposed the revolution's communist turn. The principal organized opposition emerged and settled on the island: in the Escambray Mountains, among guerrilla supporters in the countryside, and through the network of urban resistance. For a time, it threatened the survival of the revolutionary government. Or is that not the logical conclusion drawn from the massive mobilization mounted by the revolutionary government against the armed opposition? They received support from the United States of course, but the new rebels and the internal resistance were not controlled by Washington, nor had they formed at Washington's behest. Many opponents went into exile so as to better pursue the overthrow of the revolutionary government. Since the 19th century, Cuban political culture had accepted exile as a means to mobilize opposition against dictatorships. These early exiles formed the Brigade 2506 that landed at Bay of Pigs–a CIA-sponsored effort also sustained by Cuban political ideals. Throughout the 1960s, many exiled Cubans participated in CIA subversive actions on the island and abroad. Seeking Washington's or Moscow's help became a means that Cubans on either side deployed in pursuit of their respective Cuban ends, which resulted in adversaries seeing each other as simple lackeys of their respective superpowers. Yet, the root of conflict was, and is, deeply Cuban.

The organized opposition in its entirety–those who were defeated inside Cuba, endured long prison terms, and died by the thousands for the sake of their patriotic ideals, as well as those exiled groups such as Brigade 2506–constituted the other Cuba during the 1960s. The conflict between the government and the opposition–which probably qualifies as a civil war–deepened the polarization that had been building up before 1959, and that was aggravated by the radicalization of 1959-1960: the two sides fought with a rancor never before seen in Cuba. For Cubans, the 1960s became the decade of a tragic coexistence. For some, the revolution–the "era that was giving birth to a heart"–consummated independence from the United States and established the basis for a more just and, thus, more inclusive Cuba.[34] For others, the radicalization of a revolution once waged to restore democracy had yielded a dictatorship that now excluded those who did not share the goals of the top leadership. For them, total state control of the economy and the alliance with the Soviet Union were incompatible with Cuban aspirations for democracy and freedom.

In the late 1960s, violent confrontations between the government and the armed opposition began declining until it practically disappeared by the early 1970s. In 1976, the Cuban Committee for Human Rights (CCPDH) was founded by Marta Frayde, Ricardo Bofill, and others. In contrast to the initial opposition, the CCPDH issued a platform of nonviolent resistance and defense of human rights, undoubtedly influenced by the fledgling human rights movements in the Soviet Union and Eastern Europe. As with the historical opposition, the CCDPH was formed by people who had supported the revolution but broke with it due to disagreements with the top leadership. From that moment onwards and despite harsh repression, these activists slowly managed to bring increasing attention to violations of human rights in Cuba, and their efforts eventually were to be influential in the presentation of the Cuban case to the United Nations Human Rights Commission in 1991.[35] A new opposition was born in Cuba then, whose members were and continue to be dedicated to the defense of human rights, and who espouse nonviolence as their principal means of struggle.

By the early 1970s, Cuba was no longer the priority for the United States that it had been in the previous decade. Détente between the superpowers, the U.S. defeat in Vietnam, and rapprochement with China had created a new international climate. During the Gerald Ford and Jimmy Carter administrations, there was a certain easing of tensions between Washington and Havana.[36] For the most part, the exile community did not endorse this new attitude. For the traditional sector, violence was still the only valid means of opposition to the revolution, and it declared a war of sorts–"along all the world's paths"–against the Cuban government. On the one hand, the strategy responded to the diminishment of opportunities for fomenting armed resistance on the island. This "war" was intended as an answer to Havana's "internationalism" in Angola, Ethiopia, and Central America. But its targets were not only Cuban diplomats, embassies, commercial offices, and vessels; so were those exiles who advocated a nonviolent opposition, a change in U.S. policy, and contacts with Havana, or, even, those who criticized the use of violence within the United States but continued using it against the Cuban government. The exiles' "war" was consonant with traditional Cuban political culture, but it also played out in an international context where indiscriminate political violence was ascendant–from the Irish Republican Army, the *Macheteros* of Puerto Rico, and the Italian Red Brigades to the death squads in Central America. From the traditional exile community, too, came acts of abuse and crimes against fundamental rights, though now without Washington's backing,

During the 1970s, fissures first appeared in the diaspora–exiles from diverse political backgrounds sought new openings and methods. In 1976, Elena Mederos, Bishop Eduardo Boza Masvidal, and Frank Calzón founded Of Human Rights, an organization solely dedicated to denouncing political imprisonment and the human rights situation in Cuba. The Congresses of Cuban Dissident Intellectuals established links with European and Latin American intellectuals who had close ties with Eastern European dissidents that rejected violence. The Institute of Cuban Studies convened scholars, professionals, lay Catholics, and other exiles who sought exchanges with Cubans from the island. After Carter's election in 1976, the Cuban-American National Coalition opened an office in Washington to support a relaxation of U.S. sanctions. A group of young Cubans in the United States founded the magazine *Areito* (1974) and organized the Antonio Maceo Brigade (1977) as an expression of their rejection of the exile community and their support of the revolution. In 1978, the Dialogue underlined a growing pluralism among exiles.[37] The Cuban government invited some 140 people to Havana to talk about the release of 3,000 political prisoners and the opening of travel to the island by Cubans abroad. For the traditional exile community, this incipient rapprochement between Washington and Havana, as well as some exiles' participation in the Dialogue, was an unbearable affront. For traditional exiles, the possible normalization of relations between the U.S. and Cuban governments that seemed in the offing, which had the backing of some exile sectors, as well as the existence of U.S. groups openly backing the revolution, was tantamount to surrendering to Fidel Castro. Furthermore, even within traditional exile circles, tensions and differences arose regarding the use of violence in U.S. territory. For years, large segments in the exile community mistrusted dissidents in Cuba and their embrace of nonviolent resistance.

The 1970s brought significant transformations to Cuba. Domestic and foreign policies took dramatic turns: the government adopted the political and economic models then prevalent in the USSR and Eastern Europe, and Havana aligned its foreign policy with Moscow. Even though it retained a certain autonomy, the radicalism that had attracted so many in the 1960s was gone, but Havana's international profile became more pronounced–if less romantic. Domestically, the new foreign policy imposed a high cost on the citizenry. Compulsory service in military and civilian missions abroad exacted a still unknown number of lives and injuries and separated families over long periods. From the mid-1970s to the early 1980s, the economy registered acceptable growth and achieved the best living standards the regime has ever known. Nevertheless, many saw a loss of revolutionary purity and creativity in the socialist normality, à la Soviet Union and Eastern Europe, that suffused daily life. In 1980, the exodus of 125,000 people through the port of Mariel shocked Cuba. During the 1970s, the emigration escape valve had been practically closed. In 1970, the government stopped accepting applications for exit permits and, three years later, ended the air shuttle that had taken 334,000 Cubans to the United States since 1965. The leadership decided to try to integrate disaffected Cubans into the new socialist order. But visits by 100,000 Cubans from abroad in 1979, and the disappointment of people who had been kept from leaving the island after emigration policies changed in the early 1970s combined to create tensions that found an escape valve through Mariel. Thousands clamored to leave. The government organized *mítines de repudio* (repuditation meetings) in front of the homes of those who applied for exit permits and labeled them "scum." It also took the opportunity to send to the United States many insane people, as well as ex-convicts and criminals still in jails. The policy of integrating the discontented did not succeed.

In 1981, Jorge Más Canosa and other exiles founded the Cuban American National Foundation (CANF) with a new goal: securing political support in the United States for the embargo and devising new ways to confront the Castro regime. The inauguration of Radio Martí in 1985 was its paramount achievement. CANF's quick success in the Washington of Ronald Reagan proved the efficacy of the new strategy; violence as the principal opposition method against Castro slowly receded.[38] Nevertheless, CANF, Independent and Democratic Cuba (CID), and other exile organizations backed movements and governments that opposed Havana, or its allies: the Contras in Nicaragua, Jonas Savimbi and the National Union for the Total Independence of Angola (UNITA), and the different governments in El Salvador.[39] At the same time, relations with dissidents on the island were tense: exiles saw themselves as the principal opponents of the Cuban government and rejected the dialogue with official Cuba proposed by the leading dissidents. In 1987, Elizardo Sánchez Santacruz–president of the Cuban Commission of Human Rights and National Reconciliation–called for dialogue among all Cubans to bring about gradual reforms in the one-party system. In 1990, Gustavo Arcos Bergne issued a call for Castro to convene a national dialogue among all Cubans, on the island and in exile. Both proposals were harshly rejected by a great majority of the exile community.

In Cuba, the human rights movement grew and gained international recognition. In 1986, the Catholic church summoned the Cuban National Ecclesiastical Conference (ENEC), an event culminating a long process of regrouping and reflection for an institution that had been greatly weakened by its confrontations with the government in the early 1960s. ENEC exhorted the faithful to work for the common good and to seek constructive dialogue.[40] During the 1980s, young artists, intellectuals, and journalists joined in a creative movement to broaden official discourse. In general, young people and certain elite sectors were enthusiastic about the course Mikhail Gorbachev set for the Soviet Union and hoped Cuba would start its own socialist renewal. In 1989, the trial of fourteen members of the armed forces and the Interior Ministry accused of drug trafficking and the subsequent execution of General Arnaldo Ochoa, Colonel Antonio de la Guardia, and two other officers sent tremors through the elite and the population at large. Official Cuba now had little to do with the revolution of the early 1960s: if by 1970, the citizenry's initial embrace of the revolution had become "resigned support," later *la doble moral*, simulation, and political silence gradually overtook millions of Cubans.

In the section titled "Cuba's International Context in the 1990s and at the Beginning of the 21st Century," we pointed out some of the domestic issues that have hindered Cuba's international relations. The official refusal to acknowledge and respect the diversity of Cuban society has had even greater internal consequences. A series of events that took place in the 1990s are particularly important as they pertained to a sector of the population that still supported the government. In 1990, the Communist party organized meetings with its members and ordinary citizens to discuss the changes the next party congress, scheduled at the end of 1991, should make. During these meetings, people spoke up with unusual ease and frankness, a sign that, at the time, the government still retained the confidence of many Cubans. Still, when the meetings produced proposals critical of the government, the top leadership cut the discussions short. Nonetheless, consideration of reforms continued until mid-decade, albeit behind closed doors among elites. Between 1992 and 1995, in light of the demise of the Soviet Union, many party members and revolutionaries sought to persuade their leaders to reconsider their development and national security policies. From within multiple institutions, these citizens put forward their most earnest and honest efforts to open up debate about alternatives for Cuba on the eve of the 21st century, including proposals for respecting human rights and democratizing Cuban socialism.

In July 1995, however, Fidel Castro declared: "Every opening has brought us risks. If we have to open up further and make more reforms, we will do so. For the time being, these are not necessary." Some months later, the Cuban air force shot down two small planes belonging to Brothers to the Rescue, an action that cut short the political dialogue with the European Union and sped up passage of the Helms-Burton Law in the United States. At the same time, the shootdown sent an unmistakable message to those inside and outside the Communist party who strove for an internal opening and for rapprochement with the United States. In March 1996, the PCC central committee sharply delimited official debate and proposals on reforms.[41] Since then, Cuba's paralysis regarding reforms has exacted a high toll: the definitive loss of confidence in the top leadership that many party members and ordinary citizens had until then. Not a few joined or would join the Democratic Socialist Current (1992) and the Reflection Roundtable of the Moderate Opposition of Cuba (MROM, 1999).[42]

During the 1990s, the exile community continued on the path toward nonviolent opposition. The Berlin Wall crumbled, Soviet subsidies ended, and the reinforced U.S. embargo awakened hopes that Castro's final days were nearing. Indeed, so it seemed because the Cuban economy had collapsed and, in August 1994, thousands of people demonstrated at the Havana *Malecón* (waterfront) in open defiance of authorities; the government, however, dispersed the demonstrators without significant consequences.[43] That the expected change in the early 1990s did not happen–more likely than not, it would have entailed violence–reinforced the strategy of peaceful resistance. Since 1990, the Cuban Democratic Platform–a coalition group founded in 1990 by the Social Democratic Coordinating Committee, the Christian Democratic party, and the Liberal Union–has pursued peaceful change, gaining international favor and establishing links with their corresponding groups on the island. In 1993, Eloy Gutiérrez Menoyo–*comandante* of the Second Front in Escambray against Batista and later a leading Castro opponent imprisoned for 22 years–created *Cambio Cubano*, an organization committed to dialogue with the Cuban government. The Cuban Committee for Democracy was also founded in 1993 with similar purposes. The early 1990s seemed propitious for negotiations between moderate exile sectors and the Cuban government, which, in fact, were encouraged by the Europeans; unfortunately, Havana did not manifest any such disposition.

At the beginning of the 21st century, a majority of exiles acknowledge the organized opposition and human rights activists on the island as the main forces of resistance to the Cuban government, which is a sign of political maturity. Over the 1990s, exile political organizations established or widened links with different political and human rights groups in Cuba; greater communication with opponents and human rights activists in Cuba had a salutary influence on many exiles by helping them to consolidate a commitment to nonviolence. Though Miami Spanish-language radio oppose the Varela Project, a survey taken among Cubans living in South Florida showed that up to 79% support it. In an earlier poll, a majority (56%) favored national reconciliation and an amnesty for current government officials who cooperate with a democratic transition.[44]

Until the late 1970s, the breach between Cubans on the island and in exile seemed insurmountable. Not so today. Cubans on both sides of the Florida Straits have not only established political links, but have also woven a rich network of communication and contacts: e.g., family reunification visits, new migration waves, religious encounters, remittances, and cultural, academic, and professional exchanges. A growing number of diaspora Cubans are at the frontline of constructive engagement with the Cuban people. Without doubt, an insuperable political breach exists between Havana and most Cubans living abroad, and it will continue as long as the government insists on an unconditional and indistinct loyalty to Cuba, the authorities, and the maximum leader. Since 1959, however, another breach has widened–that between official Cuba and ordinary Cubans, which is also irreparable unless the government manifests a different political will.

This overview is a broad outline of the progressive political polarization in Cuba before 1959 and its subsequent worsening by the revolution's intolerance of any form of political pluralism. It is an effort to understand the Cuban past from the framework of a common civic life, independently of whether there is agreement or disagreement with every particular set forth. The ethical basis of *Cuban National Reconciliation* is respect for human rights and, therefore, the rejection of the idea that the end–laudable as it may be–justifies the means. The signatories of this report unconditionally support the statement made by Oswaldo Payá Sardiñas–initiator of the Varela Project–upon receiving the European Parliament's Sakharov Award for Human Rights in Strasbourg, France.

> Experience teaches us that violence begets more violence and that when political change is brought about by such means, new forms of oppression and injustice arise. It is our wish that violence and force should never be used as ways of overcoming crises or toppling unjust governments. This time we shall bring about change by means of this civic movement which is already opening a new chapter in Cuba's history, in which dialogue, democratic involvement, and solidarity will prevail. In such a way we shall foster genuine peace.

Cuban national reconciliation demands that a critical mass of citizens fully embrace a political ethic capable of promoting a democratic civic life–open to dialogue and respectful of pluralism–in Cuba and among all Cubans. In a letter sent to the task force from Havana, MROM leaders Manuel Cuesta Morúa and Fernando Sánchez López underscore the role of Cuban elites in national reconciliation:

> Our elites bear the greatest responsibility for bringing about reconciliation. Government elites block it by insisting on themselves as the only legitimate interpreters of common good, in spite of so much evidence to the contrary on the streets and in Cuban homes. Desperately seeking another Cuba, some emerg-

> ing elites outside official circles put forward political agendas that would entail a reinvention of Cubans as a people; others look for civilized means of communication among–past, present, and future–understanding that the nation would disappear if we insisted in reenacting our sorrows.
>
> Cubans must find civilized means of communication, which is why we understand national reconciliation as an inward effort to rebuild the balance and harmony lost through the use of different forms of violence, inequalities, injustices, and relations of domination through history.[45]

A costly legacy of polarization and absolute partisan ends has nearly overwhelmed the Cuban nation; only an exigent consensus on human rights and democracy can save it. That is the gist of the dialogue that all Cubans should heartily welcome.

## The Experiences of Other Countries

Under this heading we sketch some experiences of democratic transitions regarding past human rights violations: Spain; Argentina, Chile, and Uruguay in the Southern Cone; South Africa; El Salvador, and Guatemala in Central America; and Czechoslovakia, Albania, Bulgaria, Romania, Poland, Hungary, and Germany in Eastern Europe. Each case has its own profile of lives lost, and in each case the new democratic regimes followed specific policies to deal with these violations. *Cuban National Reconciliation* is not trying to determine whether Cuba has suffered greater or lesser human losses than other countries. The goal, instead, is to analyze how all of these losses–in Cuba and the other countries we considered–occurred when an overriding logic of absolute partisan ends opened the way for the use of violence as a means to exclude dissenters. When an end is brandished to justify assaults against the life, physical integrity, and freedoms of opponents, its nature is debased, however praiseworthy the end might seem or even if a majority supports it. What Cuba has in common with these other countries is that its government exalted absolute partisan ends that admitted no dissent. The result has been an accumulation of victims and violations–in greater or lesser numbers and intensity compared with other countries–that share the same origin: having dismissed an ethic based on human rights, which is the only means conducive to a peaceful coexistence among all citizens.

The political conditions of each transition conditioned the ways in which the new democratic governments approached the past. Perhaps the most important factor has been the way the transition took place: whether through negotiations or a sharp rupture with the preceding authoritarian regime. Since the 1970s, most transitions have been negotiated and, therefore, democratization happened from the gradual disassembling of authoritarian institutions. Transitions are more likely to initiate a profound political restructuring when the democratic opposition is strong and the dictatorial regime discredited. Their main challenge is the establishment of the rule of law, with pluralism and dialogue serving as cornerstones of civic life. To get there, a polity engages in negotiations and pacts, issues a new constitution or amends the extant one, holds free elections, strengthens civil society, and nurtures a new–or renewed–confidence of citizens in themselves and in the political system. In all cases, new democracies should resort to means that attest to their inclusiveness, and facing up to a legacy of human rights violations has constituted one of those means. Deterring future violations, identifying and sanctioning the principal violators, and restoring the victims' and/or their families' dignity, are all central considerations during a democratic transition. Though these processes–restoring silenced or absent memories and establishing the truth–should be national mandates, it must also be said that in this 21st century the search for justice is also an international concern. The following questions are of special importance in any process of recovering memory, truth, and justice:

- Was the violence overt or covert?

- At what moment of the dictatorship did it happen?

- What is the weight of the dictatorship's repressive institutions during the transition?

- What are the possibilities for identifying those responsible for the repression?

- Who are the parties interested in unveiling the violations? What actions are they taking in that regard?

A number of different mechanisms can be used in addressing a legacy of gross violations of human rights or violations of international humanitarian law. In each country, the precise manner of addressing the past will be different, and the reach, specific mandate, and character of the various initiatives that may be employed will also differ. Although the mechanisms and methodologies for achieving truth, justice, and reconciliation must be adopted according to each country's circumstances and conditions, the practices summarized here are witness to the emergence of moral and legal principles that, in effect, govern what must be done in addressing the legacy of past abuses.

With an interest in revealing the full truth about a painful and often controversial aspect of a nation's history, many countries have created a "truth commission," an official, temporary body with a mandate to investigate a pattern of abuses that took place over many years. These commissions generally operate for one to two years, finalizing their work with a public report that summarizes their findings and presents recommendations to prevent such abuses in the future. Many of these commissions have held public hearings to allow victims and other witnesses to tell their story publicly, as well as taking individual testimony from sometimes thousands of victims and investigating some of these cases in depth. In addition to official truth commissions, nongovernmental organizations have also made important contributions in collecting information from victims and publishing reports about the truth, especially where the government resists a formal truth commission. Truth commissions have generated debates concerning the search for justice because they may appear to admit impunity. Argentina, Chile, Uruguay, El Salvador, Guatemala, and South Africa are examples of countries that established these truth commissions.

A different kind of truth can emerge through the release of files kept by intelligence services of a repressive state, especially where the state closely tracked the actions of activists or dissidents over years. This release of files has taken place in some countries of Eastern Europe. There are, however, problems in using these files, as their veracity was often compromised at the time they were kept.

There is often an important need to reform the state institutions that allowed or facilitated the abuses that took place. These may include the judiciary, the police, the armed forces, and other institutions, and such reforms will typically take many years to implement fully. One important consideration is whether the individuals responsible for abuses in the past should be removed from their posts, in order to prevent further abuses and to generally strengthen those same institutions. A system of individual review of the human rights record of persons accused of abuses, which also recommends or facilitates their removal, is generally referred to as "vetting."

A different and more problematic approach to removing abusive officials is through a system of "lustration," as seen in some countries in Eastern Europe. This generally consists of removing individuals from state employ based not on each person's own individual record, but on past affiliation with a particular political party or state institution. There have been significant due process and other problems in the lustration policies as implemented in a number of countries.

An important issue that must be given close consideration in any transition is how to respond to the needs of the victims of past violence. Many countries have attempted to implement reparations for victims, including financial awards to individuals and symbolic reparations such as the construction of memorials. Such policies are critically important, although they often raise very difficult questions, especially in the attempt to provide financial reparations, as to sources of funds, how to identify the appropriate recipients, and how to fairly quantify the harm that has been done to thousands or tens of thousands of victims.

Finally, all of these countries have confronted the difficult question of whether, and in what manner, to hold persons responsible in court for past abuses. Even where there has been no amnesty granted for such acts, many countries confront the problem of a weak or overly politicized judiciary, and the fact that large numbers of people are accused of serious abuses, which makes it impossible to have a generalized prosecution system. Political conditions and pressures at the moment of transition have sometimes resulted in amnesty for some or all past abusers. In today's international context, however, amnesty for certain serious crimes is generally considered unacceptable and contrary to principles of international law, and some amnesties for human rights crimes have been overturned in domestic and international courts. The cases of South Africa and Guatemala described below are great improvements over the general and unconditional amnesties seen elsewhere in earlier years.

What follows is a précis of the experiences in other countries.

## Spain

The Spanish case is remarkable in at least two ways. First is the universally acknowledged success of its transition. After Francisco Franco's death in 1975, the new political class–integrated by the democratic opposition and Francoist reformers–and Spanish society managed a relatively peaceful passage to democracy. Still, there were more than 400 reported deaths as a result of political violence by the intransigent right and the radical left, casualties inflicted by ETA being particularly significant. By the early 1980s, Spanish democracy was well on its way. From the outset, King Juan Carlos I manifested a strong willingness for dialogue and a disposition to be inclusive, which he made plainly evident when he rose in defense of democracy to foil a coup attempt in 1981. Subsequently, the 1982 electoral victory of the Spanish Socialist Workers' Party brought to power a new generation representing political renovation and modernization. The consolidation of democracy was followed by an impressive economic boom. Doubtlessly, full integration to Europe also contributed to strengthening democracy in Spain.

The Spanish transition is also remarkable for the agreement reached by parliamentary elites not to use the past for political ends. They likewise agreed that no one would be held accountable for human rights and to implement a "let bygones be bygones" sort of policy. There was fear that uncovering the past might reenact old conflicts that could lead to a new civil war. No one wanted a repeat of the Civil War of 1936-1939. The consensus that both sides had committed atrocities during the war and that the period of Franco's harshest repression had taken place three decades earlier contributed to the decision not to account for human rights violations. Even before Franco's death, regime reformers and most of the opposition (in Spain and in exile) had agreed on a single goal for Spain: a peaceful transition to democracy.

Post-1975 negotiations were conducted with Francoist civil and military institutions intact. Between 1976 and 1978, political prisoners were set free, the Communist Party acquired legal status, legitimate elections were carried out, and a new Constitution–approved by referendum–was enacted. Tied to the negotiations was a mutual and reciprocal amnesty, which prevented the quest for justice and stymied political discussion regarding past atrocities. The transition's insistence on consensus and national reconciliation emphasized the future, not the past. Notwithstanding, sectors of Spanish society did not endorse the amnesia about the past: historians, for example, researched the Civil War and the Franco regime with almost complete freedom (with the exception of some military files still kept closed and of others that have disappeared) and published books on the subject. Political debate regarding the past, however, was not revived until recently. Notably, an exhibition, several books, and television and radio programs on the subjects of the civil war, the exiles, and Franco's regime appeared almost simultaneously in the fall of 2002. On November 20, 2002, the Spanish Parliament issued an unprecedented condemnation of the thirty-year dictatorship and extended moral recognition to the victims of the Civil War; it also made a commitment to fund the exhumation of the corpses still in common graves, both from the war and from Franco's early years in power. The parliament also acknowledged the costs imposed on those who were forced into exile during the dictatorship.

## Southern Cone: Argentina, Chile, and Uruguay

### *Argentina*

The model for truth commissions since the early 1980s originated in the Southern Cone. Argentina began the transition with a commitment to pursue truth and justice fully. Raúl Alfonsín became president after the military junta's defeat in the Falklands War in 1982; the military, thus, was doubly discredited: by the war and by the heinous repression it had sponsored since 1976.[46] In 1983, Alfonsín created the National Commission on the Disappeared (CONADEP). After nine months, the commission published *Nunca Más: The Report of the Argentine National Commission on the Disappeared*, which confirmed the disappearance of 8,963 people as well as the existence of 340 secret detention and torture centers. Since CONADEP did not publicly name repressors, some civilian organizations published a list of 1,351 individuals mentioned as such in testimonies presented to CONADEP. Courts declared unconstitutional the amnesty the military had granted themselves before leaving power. A presidential decree instructed the prosecution of military-junta members (1976-1983) and of some guerrilla leaders. At Alfonsín's behest, Congress passed a law reforming the military code of justice: if the Supreme Council of the Armed Forces did not prosecute accused military personnel within six months, the civilian justice system would bring them to trial. The law tried to limit prosecution to the higher ranking officers, but it stressed the need to administer justice where particularly "atrocious and heinous" acts had been committed. By the end of 1986, several junta members and other high-ranking officers had been prosecuted and sentenced, and it seemed as if these "trials of the century" would complete the cycle of justice.

However, that was not the case. Between 1985 and 1988, a series of events intensified the demands for justice, led the military to take action against these demands, and forced Alfonsín's government to back down. After military pressures and threats (including four failed rebellions), two laws were passed: Final Point and Due Obedience. The former established a 60-day term to register accusations against officers, and the latter limited responsibility to top leadership. Civil society, nonetheless, insisted on justice, and the judicial system responded by increasing the number of officers who could be prosecuted. Ten high-ranking officers sentenced in the mid-1980s, including five military-junta members, served up to seven years, until President Carlos Menem pardoned them in 1990. Some of them, along with many other repressors from that period, were retried in the late 1990s for the kidnapping of their victims' children. Also, lower courts declared the laws of Final Point and Due Obedience unconstitutional (as of January 2003, the Supreme Court had yet to issue a final ruling). More than thirty officers, including former president Jorge R. Videla, are still detained. Argentine justice has accepted the obligation to investigate repression during the military juntas, and since 1995 several "truth trials" have been held, although the investigations carry no penal consequences for the accused. Some of these trials have produced important revelations regarding the fate and whereabouts of some disappeared persons and the functioning of the repressive apparatus. Outside Argentina, there are pending judicial proceedings against Argentine officers for their actions during the dictatorship.

### *Chile*

From the outset, Chile's transition was constrained by the legal system put in place by Augusto Pinochet's régime and the legitimacy that the general and the military retained among certain sectors of the population. The Constitution of 1980 offered the military guarantees, even after they lost the plebiscite (1988) and the elections (1989) by 45%. Though the Coalition of Parties for Democracy won at the polls, Patricio Aylwin's government was circumscribed by legislation that bolstered the Right's power. In 1978, an amnesty absolved the army and state security of all responsibility for actions taken between 1973 and 1978.[47] Notwithstanding, the president created a truth commission to investigate political acts of violence that may have resulted in deaths or disappearances.[48] Out of 3,000 cases, the commission established the regime's responsibility for 2,025, the violent opposition for 90, and could not classify the rest.[49] In a solemn speech, Aylwin presented the commission's conclusion and, visibly moved, said the following:

> When so much suffering was inflicted by state agents, and the duly appointed state organs did not or could not prevent it or punish those responsible and neither did society take action to avert it, it is the state and society as a whole who are the ones responsible, be it for their actions or inactions. That is why–as president of the republic–speaking on behalf of the entire nation, I ask forgiveness from the families of the victims.

Subsequently, investigations on the whereabouts of the disappeared were launched. Amnesty, military autonomy, and the Right's control of the judicial system still constituted powerful barriers. Despite a vibrant human rights movement and strong democratic parties, the past got in the way of Chilean democracy.

In the late 1990s, obstacles began to give way. On the one hand, the judicial system started to lean toward human rights; many judges who had overlooked their violation during the dictatorship had retired. On the other, an international event rendered the issue of justice unavoidable. In 1998, a Spanish court initiated legal proceedings against Pinochet and other officers for the deaths of 200 people during Operation Condor.[50] After the Spanish judge Baltasar Garzón issued a warrant for Pinochet's arrest and requested his extradition to Spain, the general was arrested in London, where he remained under house arrest through the long proceedings. Moreover, English magistrates handed several unprecedented decisions confirming the principle of universal jurisdiction for massive violations of human rights. For age and health reasons, Pinochet was eventually deported to Chile. His case was brought before the Chilean Supreme Court, which revoked the immunity due him as a senator for life and prosecuted him for covering up assassinations and disappearances committed by state security agents in 1974. The Supreme Court eventually decided to stay the proceedings on the grounds Pinochet suffered from "moderate dementia." Likewise, the court developed jurisprudence allowing the investigation of disappearances and their prosecution until the victims' bodies are located or an explanation given for their having disappeared. Special judges have been appointed to investigate disappearances between 1973 and 1978, even though covered by the amnesty law. After two decades, criminal investigations are still being conducted against military officers and members of Pinochet's secret police (DINA and CNI).

### *Uruguay*

Julio María Sanguinetti's election in 1985 signaled the return of democracy to Uruguay. In 1984, the military and two out of the three principal political parties–the Colorado and the Broad Front–negotiated the transition.[51] The president was committed to what he called "pacification": repealing the State Security Act enacted by the military, returning military courts to their pre-coup jurisdiction, granting amnesty for most political prisoners, and the repatriation of exiles.[52] In Sanguinetti's estimation, the National Pacification Act–which, in addition, contained measures to aid returning exiles, former political prisoners, and those who had been fired from civil-service jobs–closed the discussion of the past.

However, other expectations arose from civil society. Human rights organizations and victims of the repression initiated legal proceedings against officers in civilian courts. A jurisdictional struggle ensued between military and civilian courts; the Supreme Court ruled in favor of civilian jurisdiction, and the investigations of hundreds of cases of human rights violations followed suit. In 1985, the congress created two commissions to investigate human rights violations during the dictatorship, but their scope was limited. The commissions established that there had been 164 disappearances and furnished the Supreme Court with evidence implicating the security forces. Not long afterwards, Peace and Justice Service (SERPAJ) organized a commission to complete what the parliamentary ones had not. In late 1986, the Uruguayan congress passed an Expiration Act declaring, "due to circumstances," an end to the state's pursuit of justice for past repression–a sort of amnesty, without terms or conditions. Victims' families, human rights organizations, and opposition sectors immediately set to work in favor of a referendum to repeal the new law. On April 6, 1989, 53 percent of the voters ratified the Expiration Act in a referendum. However, broad sectors of Uruguayan society still resent the silence, the impunity, and the fact that not even the truth of what happened has been irrefutably established. In 2000, President Jorge Batlle created a Commission for Peace and named the archbishop of Montevideo to head it; the commission has received information about disappearances in Uruguay and other countries, but has failed to obtain the collaboration of the military.

## South Africa

To date, South Africa's Truth and Reconciliation Commission (1995-1998) has been the most comprehensive and thorough. Between 1948 and 1994, apartheid–a vast system of discrimination and despotism against most of the population for the material and cultural benefit of Afrikaners and other whites–was bolstered by a powerful state apparatus that committed atrocious crimes and sowed a widespread culture of terror. The legacy of apartheid, however, is not only manifest in the atrocities committed against black South Africans (and, to a lesser degree, against Hindus), but also in the institutions and practices that exploited, silenced, and rendered the great majority destitute. Mitigating the psychological, economic, and social injustices incurred during apartheid is unquestionably more difficult than ascertaining the truth of what happened. The South African commission only investigated cases of extreme violence and, therefore, overlooked apartheid's routine humiliations and violations.

Notwithstanding, South Africa's transition materialized under relatively favorable conditions in the early 1990s: the dictatorial regime had grown politically weaker and become an international pariah, the

African National Congress (ANC) drew on impressive moral and political recourses, an exhaustive network of organizations, a proven capacity to mobilize the citizenry, and the remarkable leadership of Nelson Mandela. Parliament created the Truth and Reconciliation Commission, and nominations were put forward by the public. Mandela named the commision's seventeen members and designated Archbishop Desmond Tutu as its president. Though no conditions had been specified, an amnesty had been decided beforehand. Unlike other commissions, South Africa's had the power to grant amnesty, and it did in cases meeting three conditions: that the crimes in question took place between May 1, 1960 and May 10, 1994, that these were politically motivated, and that the accused reveal everything he or she knew about the actions involved.

The Truth and Reconciliation Commission bore an extraordinary burden: proving to the majority that the country was being founded anew on the basis of the rule of law. Although during the 1990s, prominent apartheid figures were brought to trial, they were not always condemned and not all repressors were tried; reforming the judicial system inherited from apartheid will take years. For two-and-a-half years, the commission daily exposed the monstrousness of apartheid, and that was its most important achievement. More than 21,000 victims and witnesses gave depositions; 2,000 hearings whereby the accused came face to face with the victims or their families were broadcast live on radio and television. The commission also considered accusations against ANC members, Winnie Mandela's case being the most famous. Although the commission left many victims' relatives dissatisfied, public opinion did not express a preference for justice at any cost. As expected, the Afrikaner community rejected the final report, and certain sectors demanded an unconditional amnesty. But the government of the African National Congress did not fully embrace the report either: after long discussions, it made no commitment to implement its recommendations, nor did it accept criticism of some of the methods used in the struggle against apartheid.[53]

### Central America: El Salvador and Guatemala

In El Salvador and Guatemala, transitions followed the negotiations that ended the wars between their respective governments and guerrilla forces. The peace accords called for the establishment of truth commissions. In both countries, the state was highly militarized and closely interlaced with socioeconomic élites; the repression and exclusion of a majority of citizens had been standard practice. The transition, therefore, required a deep restructuring of the state and the security forces. The cold war considerably aggravated the conflicts in El Salvador and Guatemala: after the revolution triumphed in Nicaragua, the Ronald Reagan administration allotted considerable funds to destabilize the Sandinista government and to prevent other guerrilla victories in the region; Cuba's support for Managua and for the Farabundo Martí National Liberation Front (FMLN) in El Salvador further complicated the Central American crisis. The end of the cold war and the Sandinista Front's electoral defeat in 1990 contributed to the decline of armed conflicts in El Salvador and Guatemala.

***El Salvador***

The stagnation of the war between the Salvadoran government and the FMLN hastened peace negotiations. In the late 1980s, the Nationalist Republican Alliance (ARENA)–representative of the civilian elite–took the reins of power. By then, the international community had begun to press for negotiations: the inefficiency and corruption of the Salvadoran military command, together with deeds such as the assassination of the Jesuit priests and two of their collaborators, had eroded the government's international credibility. The FMLN, in turn, joined the negotiations from a position of strength, for it had not been defeated on the battlefield. In 1992, the United Nations paved the way for the peace accord and their subsequent implementation, especially regarding the truth commission. All Salvadoran parties agreed to a U.N.-administered commission of three foreigners. An *ad hoc* commission of three Salvadorans was also named to examine the record of high-ranking military officers concerning human rights.[54]

The commission registered more than 22,000 grievances, most having to do with extrajudicial deaths, disappearances, and torture. Through the U.S. Freedom of Information Act (FOIA), important information about some of these violations was obtained.[55] Over Salvadoran government objections and with the goal of exerting pressure on the judicial system, the commission named more than 60 people (members of the armed forces, the judiciary, civil service, and the FMLN) who appeared implicated in cover ups or crimes during the conflict or who had failed to comply with their duty to investigate and punish human rights violations. In March 1993, the commission issued a report, *From Madness to Hope*, that provided evidence the armed forces and the paramilitary had been responsible for more than 85 percent of the reported violations and the FMLN for 5 percent; it was unable to assign responsibility for the remaining 10 percent. The commission recommended immediate dismissal for the officers named and a ban on holding public office for 10 years for FMLN commanders accused of abuses. Even more important, the report advocated civilian control over the armed forces, as well as comprehensive reform of the judiciary. ARENA and the military expressed sharp criticism of *From Madness to Hope,* although U.N. and U.S. pressure forced their accepting it.

All the same, a few days after the report's publication, the Salvadoran government declared an amnesty. Months later, the *ad hoc* commission concluded its review of 230 officers, and recommended transfer or removal for more than 100, including all of the top commanders. Although the Salvadoran government resisted, U.N. and U.S. pressures forced it to follow the recommendation. The officers, however, were dismissed with military honors and their pensions kept intact. In a similar fashion, the FMLN did not acknowledge any responsibility for abuses and atrocities attributed to some of its members, neither did it accept the recommendation that commanders involved in these crimes should refrain from participating in politics. Most of the victims or their families never received any compensation, nor has a monument been built in their memory, both actions having also been recommended by the commission. The transition in El Salvador was more a function of struggles among the three main elite groups–ARENA, the military, and the FMLN–as well as of international pressure; most human rights organizations did not have a say in the peace accords or their implementation. Regarding the state's demilitarization, some headway has been made as the main repressive institutions were abolished and a National Civilian Police created, drawing equally from the military and the FMLN. An independent judiciary has yet to emerge.

### *Guatemala*

Negotiations in Guatemala were conducted on different bases from those in El Salvador. In the mid-1980s, the army had practically annulled the Guatemalan National Revolutionary Union (URNG) as a military force, which meant the URNG lacked the negotiating power of the FMLN. Unlike El Salvador, the socioeconomic elite was still subordinated to the military, and the Guatemalan army did not depend on U.S. support. Moreover, the Civilian Defense Patrols (PAC), which involved the population in counterinsurgency, had no counterpart in El

Salvador. At the same time, the Catholic church and human rights organizations in Guatemala insisted on the search for the truth throughout the negotiations, and afterwards, on the application of the terms of the accords; civil society has been a vibrant player in the processes of rescuing memory and making accusations. In Guatemala, the United Nations also played an influential role.

As a result of the negotiations, the Historical Clarification Commission (CEH) was created with the purpose of investigating the truth concerning past crimes. Earlier, the Human Rights Office of the Archdiocese of Guatemala had promoted and carried out the Recovery of the Historical Memory Project (REMHI), which published the *Guatemala Never Again* report and was an important source for the official CEH. Despite these efforts, the government and the URNG agreed upon an amnesty that would not apply to those guilty of genocide, disappearances, torture, and other crimes for which there is no statute of limitations. The Catholic church's report claimed 80 percent of the violations had been committed by security forces and 9 per cent by the URNG. In 1998, the CEH issued *Guatemala: Memory of Silence*, based on the depositions of more than 8,000 people: it made a comprehensive analysis of the conflict's origins, offered irrefutable evidence of the genocide perpetrated against the Maya population, and concluded that violence had been the outcome of injustice and racism. Its recommendations included prosecuting those responsible for genocide, a wide-ranging restructuring of the military, and a far-reaching compensation program. Although there was no official contrition as in Chile, neither was there categorical denial as in El Salvador; the president and the defense minister acknowledged past "excesses," and the URNG apologized for their "mistakes." *Memory of Silence* contained a sharp critique of U.S. intervention in Guatemala since the overthrow of Jacobo Arbenz in 1954 until the late 1980s. The Clinton administration declassified some materials that proved useful to CEH; in 1999, the U.S. president set a remarkable precedent by apologizing for U.S. interference in Guatemalan conflicts.

The military is still the main political force in Guatemala and, thus, the steps taken to implement institutional and legal reforms have been feeble. However, with the dismantling of the civilian counterinsurgency patrols, progress has been made in the demilitarization of the population. The remarkable presence of civil society–with its own organizations and supported by the United Nations and nongovernmental organizations (NGOs)–has been the most distinguishing aspect of

Guatemala's transition. Recovering memory has been a powerful weapon in the hands of popular sectors. On the one hand, the initiatives to exhume corpses in clandestine cemeteries, identify the remains, present claims, and put up monuments to honor the victims have arisen from civil society–from indigenous communities to the Catholic church–with the result that the monstrousness of what happened can never be denied. On the other hand, the very act of mobilizing for these undertakings has raised the expectations of Mayan peasants regarding their rights as citizens, which is promising–albeit not a guarantee–for democracy. As in El Salvador, the elite's willingness to fully abide by the rule of law remains to be seen.

## Eastern Europe

Like Spain, the countries of Eastern Europe did not summon truth commissions to deal with their past. In general, their transitions took place with the consent of some elites from the old regimes, while Communist parties–reformed or orthodox–have been part of the political landscape since 1990. In short, Eastern Europe has seen significant continuity in its political class. Although at first public opinion favored punishing those responsible for communism, policies varied and only the former Czechoslovakia and Albania carried out extensive purges. A series of factors accounts for this relative laxity. Most important, during the 1970s, both elites and citizenry had gradually abandoned communist orthodoxy. When the regime changed, the outgoing elites were favorably positioned, especially vis-à-vis the economy, to retain some power and, in many instances, to regain it rather quickly after 1989. Moreover, the late 1940s and 1950s had been the period of harshest repression, which, by the 1980s, could be characterized as "low intensity." Accountability, thus, was no easy matter. At the same time, members of the Communist party and their families represented some 30-40 percent of the population; many citizens had passively complied with these regimes and, therefore, helped to preserve them. Finally, shortly after the transitions, economic restructuring displaced issues related to memory, truth, and justice as the public's priority concern. The past, however, has not been abandoned in Eastern Europe. On the contrary: the issues of responsibility for human rights violations are returning everywhere and are becoming more acute. Many citizens have not experienced closure with the past and are raising questions. More important, the matter of past collaboration with communist regimes is commonly used to discredit individuals in politics or with political aspirations: they are frequently "outed." There is an ongoing process of rescuing memories, building monuments, and honoring the victims of communism. Simply put, the issue is not going away.

Broadly speaking, the experience concerning the communist past is as follows:

- The former Czechoslovakia and Albania passed laws that rid the state of thousands of officials and prevented individuals closely connected with the old regime from participating in politics over a specified period.[56] In both cases, opposition parties gained power, although in Czechoslovakia lustration ("purification") against former communist officials and collaborators has been conducted according to relatively fair legal proceedings, while in Albania–the region's most repressive before 1989 and characterized for its near-lack of legal tradition–such proceedings were governed primarily by the emerging elite's political interests.

- In Bulgaria and Romania, transitions were led by communist elites, and the measures taken were symbolic. When Bulgarian communists split into orthodox and reform factions, the latter successfully blamed the former for repression and, thus, did not suffer electoral consequences when the old regime's harshness was revealed. During the 1990s, reformed communists won two national elections. In Romania, the Ceaucescus' dramatic execution did not signal rupture with communist elites. For example, the new agency for security and intelligence recruited 60 percent of its members from the former *Securitate* and, shortly afterwards, announced files would remain closed for 40 years.

- In Poland and Hungary, transition was negotiated with communist elites. For that reason and due to the complex relationships among elites during the 1990s, the past received mostly symbolic attention. In Poland, the Solidarity faction that had not been part of the first post-communist government called for justice to be done in 1991. Some groups hastily prepared lists of collaborators and pressured for legislation. The law passed in 1996 applies only to certain categories of former officials and requires them to declare whether or not they had collaborated with state security. If a special court determines an individual has not been truthful, he or she is relieved from his or her functions. The law itself, the specified categories of collaboration, and the trials, are a source of constant changes and disagreements. Though trials were few, two were quite significant: General Jaruzelski's, not for the 1981 coup d'état, but for the repression against workers' strikes in 1970; and that of a group of officers accused of mistreating political prisoners between 1945 and 1956. Trials continue into the present.

• Similarly, the Hungarian parliament enacted a law to disqualify those who had collaborated with the political police in the following ways: for having been members of the repression brigades after the Soviet invasion in 1956, or for having belonged to the political party linked with the Nazi occupation during World War II. There has, however, been little political will to follow through. The parliament also created a commission to elucidate the events of 1956, which determined that some 1,000 people had lost their lives. Hungarian politics is still polarized around the matter of what to do with those citizens who joined the Communist party and collaborated with its regime.

• Reunification sets the German case apart from the rest of Eastern Europe. East Germany was absorbed by West Germany, the latter's democratic institutions and economic prosperity having no counterpart in the region. Communist elites had no chance at all to negotiate. In reunited Germany, communists had no influence on what to do about the past. The German government allocated considerable resources to investigate the history of the German Democratic Republic (GDR). A parliamentary commission documented the GDR's functioning and declared it an illegitimate regime. By the late 1990s, the public prosecutor's office had investigated more than 62,000 cases of alleged political crimes committed under the GDR regime and had indicted more than 1,000, including former communist leader Eric Honecker and several border guards. Finally, under the supervision of Joachim Gauck, a theologian and a dissident from the East, *Stasi* files were opened to the public under strict procedures. In Germany, as well as in the rest of Eastern Europe, the use of state-security files became a delicate matter: the information in them was not always reliable and, in many cases, it was false.

Countries have employed multiple practices and methods to cope with the serious question of what to do with the past. None has found a clear answer, nor has the issue been completely settled anywhere. The countries reviewed present uneven results concerning the consolidation of democracy and their approaches toward past human rights violations. Everywhere, democracy's greatest accomplishment has been to establish a foundation of respect for the rights of citizens and a framework for the peaceful airing and settling of political differences in the public arena. All these experiences, therefore, contrast favorably and pristinely with the dictatorships that preceded them. Political and civil rights are indissolubly linked to the pursuit of all other rights.

## The Human Rights Issue in Cuba: Past and Present

The dictatorial nature of the Cuban government is now widely acknowledged. On the island, the nonviolent character and the growing number of opposition and human rights groups–the power of the powerless, in Václav Havel's words–have brought the regime's true character to light. The history of human rights violations, however, does not have the same level of recognition and, in fact, remains, largely unknown. The Cuban revolution's vital role in the New Left movement of the 1960s and the support it elicited from progressive and leftist intellectuals partly explains this lacuna. There are, however, other reasons. In the 1960s, democracy was mainly confined to Western, developed countries and, even there, some dictatorships survived in southern Europe. In the Third World, right-wing dictatorships perpetrated horrific repression in the name of fighting communism, almost always with open or tacit U.S. support. The profile of the international human rights community that emerged after the Helsinki Final Act also had an impact: until the 1980s, its activists tended to be left of center. In the United States, the lobby on behalf of human rights arose in opposition to, and in denunciation of, U.S. policies that subverted democratic governments and supported military regimes; due to U.S. hostility towards Cuba, the situation on the island did not receive much attention. Moreover, when the human rights international movement flourished during the 1970s, the cruelest period of repression in Cuba until that time was over. While during the 1960s the Cuban government silenced the organized opposition through violence, long prison terms, and firing squads, repression by the 1970s more commonly, but not exclusively, took the form of intimidation, harassment, arbitrariness, and imprisonment. Finally, many exiles–the first to denounce the Cuban government–were not natural allies of the human rights activists: most sided with the United States in the cold war, largely shared the anticommunist ideology of right-wing regimes and, therefore, overlooked violations committed by these regimes. A double standard impregnated the human rights issue in relation to Cuba: on the one hand, important sectors of the international community did not give Cuban victims the same consideration as victims of right-wing dictatorships, the Soviet Union, and Eastern Europe; on the other, many exiles did not condemn right-wing dictatorships nor recognize their victims.[57]

A combination of factors has partly corrected the way the international community approaches human rights in Cuba: the absolutist character of the Cuban government, the expansion of an independent civil society on the island, as well as the international consensus on democracy and human rights. Even so, the international community focuses mostly on the current status of human rights on the island and demands the Cuban government respect them. *Cuban National Reconciliation* considers another aspect to be important: the human cost exacted by the revolution, especially but not exclusively during the 1960s, and also, by the violent opposition, albeit to a lesser extent. The 1960s was the decade of civil conflict and tragic coexistence, and Cubans should shed as much light as possible on those events then so that similar ones never happen again in Cuba.

All sides in the Cuban conflict have justified their actions, appealing to a logic of absolute partisan ends. This report, however, embraces respect for human rights–an ethics of means–as the unmovable cornerstone for civil coexistence. Even though current conditions in Cuba are not ripe for clarifying the past, *Cuban National Reconciliation* recommends doing what is feasible: creating a framework for a discussion of what happened in light of international agreements and norms on human rights, including:

- The International Bill of Human Rights, which includes the Universal Declaration on Human Rights, as well as the International Covenant on Civil and Political Rights and its optional protocols.

- The American Declaration of the Rights and Duties of Man, the American Convention on Human Rights, and the Inter-American Convention to Prevent and Punish Torture.

- The Convention against Torture and Other Cruel, Inhuman, or Degrading Treatment or Punishment, which includes basic principles for the treatment of convicts and protection against forced disappearances.

- The four conventions (1949) and the two protocols of Geneva (1977), as well as UN and OAS agreements on humanitarian international law, protection of civilians during wars, proper treatment of war prisoners, the inapplicability of statute of limitations to war crimes and crimes against humanity, as well as the rights and duties of states in the event of civil conflicts.

• The proscriptions of the International Labor Organization (ILO) in relation to forced labor.

• The United Nations has sponsored 12 multilateral conventions that classify as terrorism actions such as kidnapping of, or attacks against, planes or ships, assaults against officials and diplomats, taking hostages, and financing terrorism.

International law provides an ethical and legal framework that does not accept many of the arguments used to justify what happened in Cuba by the Cuban government, by the violent opposition, or by the U.S. government. Looking forward to a democratic Cuba with the goal of a pluralistic quest for truth, we note the following, which is a compilation of facts, issues, allegations, and questions that should be considered, investigated, and determined. The full range of what happened in Cuba has yet to come to light.

**Cuban Government Violations and Related Issues in Need of Clarification**[58]

• Massive violations of citizen rights and individual freedoms as per the severe restrictions sanctioned by the constitution and the criminal code.

• Post-1959 extension and application of the death penalty to politically motivated actions. How many people were brought before firing squads?

• Imposition of sentences–including, especially in the 1960s, the death penalty and unusually long prison terms–in trials that did not and still do not abide by internationally established standards of due process.

• Determination of the number of political prisoners since 1959. How many were or are condemned for acts of political violence? How many were or are prisoners of conscience?

• Mistreatment of political and common prisoners. Deliberate confinement in prisons far removed from their families. Tortures–physical and psychological–and extrajudicial deaths from 1959 until the present. Clarification of the situation at the Isle of Pines prison (approximately 5,000 prisoners) which was mined with live dynamite between January 1962 and February 1963. Clarification of the situation at Boniato prison (1976), when at least one person died and dozens were beaten up.[59]

• Identification of the whereabouts of all those killed for political reasons and the return of their remains to their families. Furnishing families with accurate information of how their loved ones died.

• Use and abuse of preventive arrest for political reasons. On the eve of the Bay of Pigs invasion, the government arrested thousands.[60] Current application of this policy against the organized opposition and human rights activists.[61]

• Treatment given to prisoners of war: members of Brigade 2506 in 1961 and the rebels in Escambray and other areas during the 1960s. Torture and extrajudicial killings.

• Human rights violations of civilians living in war zones, particularly the forced relocation of peasants from Escambray to newly created, far-removed "communities." How many people were relocated? How many "communities" were created? How long did these exist? Where were they?

• Forced labor as punishment for behavior considered improper by the state, such as political dissidence, religious beliefs, sexual preference, or inclination to delinquency, e.g., the Military Units to Aid Production (UMAP), and for persons who had applied to leave Cuba. How many people were sent to UMAP or forced to work against their will?

• Number of HIV positive people, or people already suffering from AIDS, who were forcibly confined and isolated in special clinics.

• Establishing accurately the number of Cubans who died in international missions, especially during the war in Angola.[62]

• How many people have died from being intercepted by Cuban authorities as they attempted to leave the country on rafts or boats? The deliberate sinking of the tugboat *13 de marzo* in July 1994 has been the most notorious in recent times. Forty-one people, including ten minors, lost their lives.

• The shootdown of two civilian aircrafts over international waters on February 24, 1996.

• Were agents of the Cuban government involved in some of the violence perpetrated in exile communities?

Regarding some of these issues, the Cuban government has issued a kind of oblique acknowledgement. Ramiro Valdés' removal as interior minister in 1968 could be partly attributed to the situation of political prisoners.[63] His successor, Sergio del Valle, implemented a so-called progressive plan that shortened sentences and gradually freed many political prisoners through a work program in construction, agriculture, and other civilian activities. The plan's mere implementation was an implicit recognition that political imprisonment under then-existing conditions could no longer be sustained.[64] The progressive plan, however, did not solve the situation of the prisoners who refused to participate in it for reasons of conscience–they continued as *plantados*–and whom the authorities treated with particular harshness.[65] Regarding the peasant population, Carlos Rafael Rodríguez recognized government policies were not always "properly applied," saying that "serious mistakes had been made in relations with the peasantry," and that "revolutionary legality was not respected."[66] With respect to UMAP, a story in the party newspaper, *Granma*, noted the following:

> Upon arrival of the first groups, which were no good, some officers did not have enough patience, nor did they have the required experience and overreacted. That is why their cases were submitted to a *Consejo de Guerra* (war council); some were demoted, others dismissed from the armed forces.[67]

During a conference held in 2001 for the 40th anniversary of the Bay of Pigs invasion, a Cuban government official acknowledged it had been a "mistake" to transport dozens of war prisoners in an unventilated tractor trailer; nine men asphyxiated on the trip, which took several hours.[68] Though welcomed, these readings and clarifications are but grains of sand in what should be a wide and transparent sea, so neither this nor any future government in Cuba ever acts that way again. Indeed, the experiences of other countries highlight the significance of restoring memory, unveiling the truth, and pursuing justice in order to identify the guilty and determine their criminal and political responsibility. Due process, and the presumption of innocence until proven otherwise in properly conducted trials, should guide these processes, which should never be construed as witch hunts.

### The Violent Opposition's Abuses, Crimes, or Atrocities, and Related Issues in Need of Clarification

- The victimization of civilians and the assaults on civilian installations by the urban internal resistance, the rebels in Escambray and other areas, as well as from exiles, in their actions against the government. Clarification of the cases of teachers and peasants killed by the rebels in Escambray and other areas, and of the civilian casualties that resulted from intermittent attacks by exiles against Cuban coastal towns and installations.

- The treatment given to prisoners of war held by rebels in Escambray and other areas.

- The attacks against Cuban diplomatic missions and commercial offices abroad, including Cuba's U.N. mission and *Cubana de Aviación* offices in several countries.

- The attacks against Cuban fishing or merchant-marine ships in open sea.

- The 1976 explosion of a *Cubana de Aviación* flight from Barbados, which killed 73 people.

• The assassination or kidnapping of Cuban diplomats in Portugal, Argentina, Mexico, and the United States, as well as the murder of a former minister in Salvador Allende's government.

• The attacks in Miami against travel agencies and other businesses with Cuban links in the late 1970s and early 1980s, against the businesses and homes of some supporters of a *rapprochement* with the Cuban government, and against individuals who opposed the traditional exile's line, as well as against sectors of the exile community who condemned the use of violence in U.S. soil.

• The assassination of persons in Miami, New Jersey, and Puerto Rico who favored new tactics in the struggle against the Cuban government, an openness with Havana and/or a new U.S. policy towards Cuba, as well as against individuals who were part of the traditional exile community.

During the 1960s, many actions against the Cuban government involved the United States, in different ways and levels. The planning and implementation of many more was done by Cubans and, therefore, the responsibility for their consequences is also Cuban. It is crucial to determine which human losses were caused by Cuban actions in the civil confrontation and which resulted from U.S. initiatives. The revolutionary government had a genuine and autochthonous Cuban opposition and the actions of that opposition, even its possible abuses, crimes, or atrocities, have to be so attributed. In 1999, the Cuban government filed a claim, "The People of Cuba vs. the Government of the United States of America for Human Damages," which does not acknowledge the Cuban opposition as an autonomous actor.[69] Under international law, the violence perpetrated against Cuban government targets abroad, and against those Cubans in exile who favored another policy towards the island, or who simply did not support the use of violence in U.S. territory, can only be considered terrorism.

Regarding the abuses that members of the armed opposition perpetrated in Cuba during the 1960s, many of those responsible are likely to have already suffered consequences–they were brought before firing squads or served long prison terms. In some cases of violence by exiles, trials have been conducted and sentences dictated.[70] Since *Cuban*

*National Reconciliation* places such an emphasis on traditional political culture, it considers it important to note that recent developments among exiles reveal a transformation already in progress. A person who spent more than four years in jail for refusing to testify before a New York grand jury convened to investigate Cuban exile violence expressed the following about the changes he underwent while in confinement:

> When I left prison, I made the commitment to myself and my brethren in this struggle to disseminate a philosophy of nonviolent civic struggle, to work according to its ideas, not just as a matter of strategy, but as a principle for living and struggling.[71]

Whatever his activities before being jailed, upon his release he steered other young Cubans away from violence and toward peaceful means to oppose Castro. Even so, it is impossible to underestimate the prejudicial effects that the violence perpetrated in exile, mainly in Miami, and the warrior mentality that still prevails in some sectors, have had on freedom of expression in Cuban Miami's public discourse. However, it is also impossible to argue that Cuban Miami is the same in 2003 as it was 15 or 20 years ago.[72] A prominent member of the Cuban American National Foundation noted the following about the climate that long prevailed in Miami:

> For too many years, many of us kept quiet when the motives of our fellow citizens were questioned. To those who suffered because of it, I ask for forgiveness for not having spoken out more forcefully. From now on, I'll refuse to play that game, and will not diminish another person who fights for freedom.[73]

In turn, the president of Brothers to the Rescue president expressed his approval of sending humanitarian aid to Cuba after hurricane Michelle in November 2001:

> The material value of our aid, given all that Cuba needs, would not give Castro a single additional day in power. The benefit Castro could draw from the aid sent by exiles carries no real political cost to our cause. We only imagine it so.
>
> Showing human solidarity does not imply weakness…If we give generously, we will have achieved a great moral victory before

> our people and the world, with a small material and insignificant cost as far as helping the regime is concerned. Yet, if we do not provide our assistance, our fellow citizens would judge us indolent, and, in the opinion of third parties, we would again be acting intransigently in the face of a tragedy that should concern us all. We have fallen into this trap before.[74]

In February 2003, CANF's president underscored the need for dialogue among all Cubans in order to jointly find a solution to Cuba's problems.

> Cuba and its destiny belong to all Cubans with the will to be free, to take off existing chains, and to walk towards the light. We need to walk down that road together, those who are in Cuba and those abroad, young and old people, the intransigent and the benevolent... Let's not be afraid of talking to each other, of a conversation among Cubans, of looking for the road to peace, freedom, and progress together.[75]

Since the mid-1990s, progress has been made toward a more pluralistic, open, and inclusive community, though more work is needed to arrive at a truly civic conscience that values dialogue and an ethic of means in the diaspora.

**U.S. Government**

Operation Mongoose has been widely documented.[76] The CIA mounted an extensive network of covert actions against strategic targets–military and civilian–with the purpose of overthrowing the Cuban government. Many of the most serious actions against civilian facilities in Cuba were initiated and financed by the U.S. government; most were implemented by members of the Cuban opposition, not a few of whom had been trained by the CIA. Even if direct U.S. participation was minor, Washington's responsibility for initiating and financing many actions, as well as for training many individuals to carry them out, is clear in the sources that have come to light through the Freedom of Information Act. The U.S. government has already acknowledged a series of significant events.

- The CIA's participation in attempts against Fidel Castro's life.

In 1975, under the direction of Democratic Senator Frank Church, the U.S. Senate Committee for Intelligence Affairs conducted extensive hearings regarding possible CIA participation in plots to assassinate foreign leaders. The evidence submitted corroborated eight specific plans to eliminate the Cuban leader between 1960 and 1965, though some went no further than the planning stage; no other such attempts by the U.S. government have been corroborated.[77] Church wrote the following in the preface to the report published by the Senate committee he presided:

> We regard the assassination plots as aberrations. The United States must not adopt the tactics of the enemy. Means are as important as ends. Crisis makes it tempting to ignore the wise restraints that make men free; but each time we do so, each time the means we use are wrong, our inner strength, the strength which makes us free, is lessened.[78]

In 1975, President Gerald Ford signed an executive order prohibiting U.S. government agencies from resorting to assassination in the conduct of foreign policy and the defense of national interests.

The official Cuban claim for human damages also alleges the following:

- In 1981, the U.S. government introduced in Cuba the virus that causes hemorrhagic dengue type 2; the epidemic took the lives of 158 people, 101 of whom were children.

The Cuban government's accusation regarding the deliberate introduction of this virus should be duly investigated. Sectors of public opinion on the island believe this allegation to be true, hence, a prestigious and independent entity should determine its veracity or lack thereof.

Once the transition begins, *Cuban National Reconciliation* believes the U.S. government should fully cooperate with Cuban authorities and civil society in order to elucidate as accurately as possible all the issues relating to U.S. foreign policy towards the Cuban government since 1959, especially those issues that had human costs. A democratic Cuba deserves the same consideration given to El Salvador and Guatemala by the Clinton administration for the sake of establishing the greatest transparency possible in the new relationship that Cuba and the United States would then have to forge.

## National Reconciliation

Reconciliation cannot be dictated nor decreed. It is, on the contrary, a long, multi-faceted process that can be duly consolidated only under the rule of law. We strive for a necessary and sufficient level of reconciliation so that all Cubans–on the island and abroad–may live in peace, that is to say, in a democracy with strong institutions supportive of peaceful resolutions to political differences. A platform of reconciliation recognizes the pluralism of Cuba as a nation, and that such diversity nourishes its patrimony. So that all voices may be heard in the arena of public discourse, Cubans must cling to a civic ethics that compels them to listen and to dialogue; no group, sector, or person has a monopoly on truth, and dialogue often changes people's minds. Librado Linares García, coordinator of the Cuban Reflection Movement, said as much in a letter to the Task Force from Camajuaní, Villa Clara:

> Only a reasoned reconciliation, not vindictive...would ensure the creation and consolidation of a new national project, as well as the proper development of a pro-democracy movement that becomes a true counter-power, could ensure that the actual regime does not survive in the future. My position is clearly on behalf of reconciliation. However, the way such reconciliation is implemented will be determined by debate in the public arena, and all actors should be there.[79]

Signs of a reinvigorated civic ethics can already be seen in Cuba: in independent civil society, in the flourishing of faith-based communities, in independent intellectual expression, in the courage shown by those imprisoned for reasons of conscience, in the integrity of those who have raised human rights as the unquestionable bastion of their civic and political life, imagining a democratic Cuba where the opposition would never be harassed as it is today.

Reconciliation requires an understanding of the polarization that tore Cuba apart, as well as a recognition and a commitment by the great majority of Cubans that it should never happen again. Upon reaching such understanding, recognition, and commitment, Cubans will have overcome the warrior mentality–a reflection of polarization–that still marks their political rhetoric. There are, however, indications of change. Unusual but notable was the use of the term "invaders" (instead of the established "mercenaries") by the Cuban media to refer to the five

Brigade 2506 veterans who attended a conference on the Bay of Pigs' 40th anniversary. Recently, Miami has given multiple indications of openness: e.g., the Cuban-community support of the Varela Project even though its starting point is the Constitution of 1976; the establishment of a scholarship at Miami-Dade Community College in honor of singer Elena Burke, who lived and died in Cuba; public opinion polls that indicate more open and inclusive attitudes among South Florida Cubans; and the civil debates on the embargo between two Cuban-American candidates for a congressional seat in 2002. Manuel Cuesta Morúa and Fernando Sánchez López–MROM promoters–also take note of similar changes in Cuba:

> Behind their harsh and absolute discourse, Cubans find reconciliation within their families, in religion, in culture, in a healthy attempt to reach minorities, and in their informal, but powerful claim to be recognized as individuals. Before these facts, intolerance evaporates: and intolerance is the cultural fuel of our historical machinery of violence...
>
> To counter the negative consequences of violence–psychological, physical, or verbal–reconciliation should start with an ethical vindication and a practical moralization of the main instruments of politics: dialogue, negotiation, transactions, and pacts...Dialogue at the social and political level and forgiveness at the moral level constitute possibilities for a successful reconciliation.[80]

Payá's message at the European Parliament is clear and conclusive:

> Cuba's civic combatant heroes–the ordinary people who have signed the Varela Project– carry no weapons. Not a single hand is armed. We walk with both arms outstretched, offering our hands to all Cubans as brothers and sisters, and to all peoples of the world. The first victory we can claim is that our hearts are free of hatred. Hence we say to those who persecute us and who try to dominate us: "You are my brother. I do not hate you, but you are not going to dominate me by fear. I do not wish to impose my truth, nor do I wish you to impose yours on me. We are going to seek the truth together." This is the liberation we are proclaiming.

> There are still those who perpetuate the myth that there is conflict between the exercise of political and civil rights and a society's ability to achieve social justice and development. They are not mutually exclusive. The absence of any civil and political rights in Cuba has had serious consequences, such as inequality, the poverty of the majority and privileges of a minority, and the deterioration of certain services, even though these were conceived as a positive system to benefit the people.

Even though the path imposed by official Cuba is not the way, within its ranks there are a good many people doubly capable–for their talents and because they will use that talent to ease the transition to democracy and national reconciliation. There were, and there are, Cubans of good will, of personal and professional integrity, on both sides. In a recently published article, Dagoberto Valdés Hernández–a lay Catholic from Pinar del Río and editor of *Revista Vitral*– provides a sharp analysis that should be embraced by all honest Cubans, wherever they may physically or politically be, because a future in peace cannot be built on the basis of the present.

> Something is moving in Cuba. More and more often, we see political paralysis as the patrimony of the power structure, and we note that initiatives of all types characterize the incipient civil society, and the simple citizens who choose to remain here and to open up different spaces for participation.
>
> We should look beyond our day-to-day-survival and, for a moment, consider how far we have come. Hiding what moves, so that those who have managed to move a bit are discouraged, is the first trick paralysis plays. Franco, the Spanish dictator, used to say: "Whoever moves will not come out in the photograph." That is to say, whoever moves disappears, does not exist, does not count.
>
> We should look ahead. This is the way I look at things, and I share it with the purpose of contributing an opinion that not only looks ahead, but also and above all, that helps raise the self-esteem of those citizens who seriously assumed their responsibility as protagonists (which means "first in agony"), that is to say, that helps those who have opted for sacrifice, for serving

others, giving much of themselves, sacrificing their families and safety for the nation all Cubans constitute.[81]

*Cuban National Reconciliation* considers helpful to delimit four main aspects of a reconciliation process.

• Reconciliation of Every Cuban with Himself or Herself

There are enough reasons–on one side or the other–for the wounds and pain accumulated for all that has happened since 1959. No one has a right to ask victims to forgive and reconcile with oppressors. All Cubans, however, have the right to expect a social context that allows them to leave their children and grandchildren a Cuban homeland that is strongly protected by institutions and rights and, therefore, has banished political violence. Rancor and vengeance cannot set the guidelines for their national reunion. Restoring silenced or absent memories, unveiling truths, and seeking justice may be helpful so that each individual–victims and oppressors, Cubans on one side or the other–may make peace with himself or herself and with the past, so that all can look forward with only one weapon in hand: a civic conscience of citizen rights and responsibilities.

• Family Reconciliation

Within families, reconciliation has advanced the most. It started in the late 1970s with family reunification travel and has continued ever more deeply and irreversibly. During the 1990s, family links increased due to the frequency of travel–the numbers of people who went to Cuba and the numbers of Cubans from the island who visited their relatives in the diaspora–as well as the remittances from the diaspora to their families in Cuba. In spite of the political context, Cuban families have practically left politics behind as a reason of discord and separation.

• Reconciliation in the Diaspora

During the 1970s, the emerging pluralism–regarding the embargo, the use of violence as the principal means of opposition, and the opening towards the Cuban government–shattered the consensus that had characterized the exile community. These issues generated intense polemics that–suffused with a warrior mentality on all sides–did not constitute a dialogue. Though Cuban Miami today has left political violence behind, civic life in the diaspora still requires care and attention. Cubans abroad–especially in Miami–have the responsibility to make their discourse ever more civic, open, tolerant, and inclusive. Reconciliation in the diaspora is within reach and requires all political currents to make an effort to express their differences in such a way as to leave the warrior mentality behind. Only then will a true dialogue begin. If it happens, this reconciliation would demonstrate the ability of Cubans in the diaspora–who are also part of Cuba and have rights and duties regarding democratization and reconciliation–to coexist civilly.

• Political Reconciliation

In the longer run lies a reconciliation based on a new pact agreed upon among political actors and with Cuban society, which will raise an ethics of means–respect for human rights–as the basic, unmovable cornerstone of politics. For this pact to come to life in Cuban society, it will have to be sustained by a civic conscience regarding duties and rights of the citizenry. Then, the public arena will be protected by a state founded upon an ethics that upholds the rights of citizens to dissent, using their own and autonomous means, without fearing reprisals. Only then will there be room for all. When that happens, we will be able to say that Cubans are living in peace.

Because it will be a long process, reconciliation will take place one step at a time. As the poet Antonio Machado said: "Wayfarer, there is no path, you make the path as you go." However, we end this report with the hope that, some day, a promising and memorable ceremony of national reconciliation will be celebrated. The Escambray Mountains would be a good place for a solemn act to honor the memory of all Cubans who have fallen victim to political violence since 1959. There, Cubans could unveil a monument engraved with the names of each and every one of those dead, from one side and the other. Veterans of the civil conflict from both sides would participate in the ceremony, which would truly be a moment of harmony. In Trinidad, at the foot of the Escambray Mountains, the museum that now documents "The Struggle Against Bandits" would be modified: it would integrate memories from all sides so that it would offer an all-encompassing history of what by then may be called a civil war.

Should these things come to pass, Cuba would be on the right path, perhaps once and for all. With that new vision for the Cuban nation in our minds and in our hearts, we offer readers the report, *Cuban National Reconciliation.*

# Endnotes

1. In international law, the expression "human rights violations" refers to those government actions that may qualify as such; the terms "abuses, crimes, or atrocities" refer to the actions of a violent opposition that do not abide by humanitarian law. When such an opposition commits atrocious crimes, as would be the case in war crimes and crimes against humanity, the term used is "international crimes." To facilitate its reading, this report uses the term "violations" to refer to the Cuban government and "abuses, crimes, or atrocities" to refer to the armed opposition. The distinction underscores the greater responsibility of governments as regards human rights–for their protection and in their breach.

2. This report understands the internationally established difference between political opponents and human rights activists. We have generally abided by this difference regarding Cuba, even though, on the one hand, the government considers human rights activists opponents, while on the other, many activists are also members of political organizations.

3. Obviously, the Soviet Union and Eastern Europe never implemented reforms to mitigate the lack of civil and political freedoms, as did Western democracies with respect to social and economic rights through the welfare state.

4. Although the Cuban government was expelled in 1961, the Organization of America States (OAS) considers the Cuban state a member and, consequently, claims the right to see that hemispheric norms are respected in Cuba. Between 1962 and 1983, the Inter-American Commission on Human Rights issued seven reports on the Cuban situation. In subsequent years, the IACHR has published a chapter in its annual report that analyzes the situation of human rights in Cuba.

5. Under international treaties and norms agreed upon after World War II, there is no moral or legal justification for violations of human rights. Economic sanctions and punitive restrictions on commerce are, in general, procedures also forbidden by international law. Nevertheless, in certain circumstances, exceptions are made.

6. In 1994, the Cuban government opened the island's coastline and, consequently, some 35,000 people left the country on rafts. Once at sea, the U.S. Coast Guard intercepted them and took them to Guantánamo Naval Base. Less than a year later, the *balseros* (rafters) were allowed to enter the United States legally. Prior to the 1994 pact, there were three migration agreements–1965, 1984, and 1987. Since 1994, Washington and Havana have held regular contact on the migration issue.

7. Although Havana still has the highest concentration of nonviolent civil actions, these have extended to all the provinces. Five years ago the organized opposition was made up of just a few political groups; in 2002, there was an increasing network of independent social institutions, e.g., libraries, journalists, and unions. Likewise, the means of communication among opponents have expanded and become more efficient. The human rights organizations and activists have also increased their activity. *Pasos a la libertad 2001* (Miami: Directorio Democrático Cubano and Centro de Estudios para Una Opción Nacional, 2002).

8. Since 1992, the General Assembly has been approving resolutions against the embargo. Between 1992 and 1998, it also issued annual resolutions in reference to the human rights situation in Cuba. The UN Human Rights Commission has also rejected unilateral coercive measures, on the grounds these prevent the full realization of all the rights enunciated in the Universal Declaration of Human Rights. See: "Human Rights and Unilateral Coercive Measures," Resolution of the Human Rights Commission, November 2000.

9. The Vatican presented a list of over 300 prisoners (political and common), of which 106 had already been freed. The government liberated approximately 200 more people. In all, some 150 were, or had been, political prisoners.

10. The Latin American countries that voted in favor of the resolution were: Argentina, Chile, Costa Rica, Mexico, Peru, and Uruguay. The commission also asked the United Nations High Commissioner for Human Rights to send a personal representative so that the Office of the High Commissioner seek Cuban government cooperation in the resolution's implementation.

11. Between 1993 and 1998, Special Rapporteur Carl-Johan Groth issued annual reports to the UN Human Rights Commission and the United Nations General Assembly on the situation of human rights in Cuba. Ambassador Groth's reports served to encourage human rights activists in Cuba to document and report violations. By giving publicity to serious human rights violations committed by the Cuban government, the reports also extracted a political cost from Cuba in the eyes of the international community.

12. The United Nations International Civil Aviation Organization determined the aircrafts were shot down over international waters. Founded in 1991, Brothers to the Rescue has had flying over the Florida Straits in search of rafters as one of its objectives; between 1991 and 1996 it carried out some 2,400 missions and rescued some 4,200 people. The organization is also committed to helping the nonviolent opposition on the island; prior to this tragic incident, its planes had flown over Cuban territory dropping anti-Castro leaflets. Brothers to the Rescue adheres to nonviolent civil disobedience, and their pilots did not carry weapons. Before February 24th, the Cuban government had explored the possibility of taking drastic measures against the planes that made incursions into their air space with several high-ranking U.S. visitors who warned the consequences for U.S.-Cuban relations would be disastrous.

13. In 2000, the U.S. Congress approved the sale of food and medicine to Cuba without permitting their financing by U.S. public or private institutions. The first food purchase was negotiated at the end of 2001, and the Cuban government paid in cash. In September 2002, a fair of U.S. agricultural products was held in Havana. Nearly 300 companies participated, 34 of which were from Florida.

14. Examples of some of the proposed political reforms were: separation of functions (having different people hold the presidency and the office of Communist Party general secretary), creation of the office of prime minister, and incorporation of some opposition members to the National Assembly. The legalization of small- and medium-sized private business was at the heart of the delayed economic reforms.

15. The four signatories to *La Patria es de Todos* sought to answer the document then circulating among Communist Party members in prepa-

ration for the party congress that would be held in October 1997. The four were sentenced to between two-and-a-half to five years in prison. Just before former President Carter visited Cuba in May 2002, Vladimiro Roca Antúnez became the last of the group to be released.

16. The Varela Project proposes a referendum on five issues: the right to freedom of expression, the right to freedom of association, a partial amnesty for political prisoners, the right of Cubans to start their own businesses, and a new election law.

17. Norberto Fuentes, *Cazabandido* (Montevideo: Libros de la Pupila, 1970), p. 26. Marcelina and her husband José Tartabull had nine children: three of them–José Esteban, Evangelisto, and Javier–enlisted in the militias; one of them–Rigoberto–joined the rebels in Escambray. José Esteban and Rigoberto died in combat. Their parents put a photograph of each in the same frame and hung it at the entrance of the house where they were born and raised. The frame was draped in red, blue, and white, the colors of the Cuban flag.

18. Machado carried out the fiercest repression in republican Cuba up to that moment. His opponents resorted to what now would be characterized as terrorism: indiscriminate violence in places where the risk of civilian casualties was high.

19. The Platt amendment was appended to the 1901 Constitution and recognized the right of the Unites States to intervene in Cuba when its political stability was endangered. Washington imposed it as a condition to withdraw the occupation begun in 1898, at the end of the Cuban War of Independence (1895-1898) and the conflict between Spain and the United States (1898). Under the amendment, several and varied interventions took place: e.g., a second occupation (1906-1909), a civilian interference (1919–1922) regarding administrative honesty and state budgets, and a mediation between the government and the organized opposition led by U.S. Ambassador Sumner Wells (1933). In 1934, the amendment was abolished by President Franklin Delano Roosevelt's administration. The Platt amendment is a symbol that still mobilizes some nationalist sectors against the United States.

20. *Bohemia*, June 29, 1941.

21. Quoted from a letter written by Alberto Müller Quintana, general secretary of the Revolutionary Student Directorate, to newly inaugurated U.S. president, John F. Kennedy, on January 24, 1961, from the underground in Cuba. Müller had been a student leader against Batista and again against Castro. He was arrested in 1961 and spent 15 years in prison.

22. The Revolutionary Directorate opposed Batista via armed struggle. In March 1957, it organized an unsuccessful assassination attempt against the dictator, which took the life of its principal leader, José Antonio Echevarría. In early 1958, a Directorate faction established a guerrilla unit in the Escambray Mountains, known as the Second Front. The Directorate and the Second Front were independent from the July 26 Movement.

23. A majority of the Task Force on Memory, Truth, and Justice considers the conflict between the revolutionary government and the organized opposition to have constituted a state of civil war. Nevertheless, we prefer not to use the term definitively in deference to the future reflection that should take place–in Cuba and among all Cubans–based on a rigorous analysis of the facts and the programs of the groups that clashed between 1960 and 1966.

24. Figures for rebel groups and militias can be found in Raúl Castro, "Discurso pronunciado en la graduación del III curso de la escuela básica superior, 'General Máximo Gómez'", *El Orientador Revolucionario*, 17 (1967): 11. The same source mentions the existence of 3,591 rebels. The figure of 8,000 appears in a document declassified by the Ministry of the Interior as part of a package for a conference on the Bay of Pigs invasion in March 2001. When Jorge I. Domínguez asked about the difference in the two figures, the former Interior Minister Ramiro Valdés replied that the correct figure was given in 1967. The number of casualties was taken from Enrique Encinosa, *Escambray, la guerra olvidada*. Miami: Editorial Sibi, 1988, p. 19. In the cited 1967 speech, Raúl Castro acknowledged the loss of 500 militias. Since we currently do not have the means to verify them, these figures will all have to be credibly established.

25. The figure of 12,000 soldiers in Batista's army appears in Jorge I. Domínguez, *Cuba: Order and Revolution*. Cambridge: Harvard

University Press, 1978, p. 126. Hugh Thomas in *Cuba: The Pursuit of Freedom*. New York: Harper & Row Publishers, 1971, p. 1.042, considers various sources on the Rebel Army and concludes the total of up to 2,000 is correct for the end of 1958. According to Thomas (p. 1.044), Ramón Grau San Martín was the first to quote the famous total of 20,000 dead during the 1950s in an interview granted to *The New York Times*; early in 1959, the media repeated the 20,000 total which was quickly assumed by the official discourse. After analyzing different sources, Thomas suggests the total probably did not exceed 2,000. In the future, a rigorous historical investigation should be conducted in Cuba to document the total number of victims during the Batista regime. Two types of questions need to be determined: the cause of death–in battle, from abuses suffered as political or war prisoners, and through violence against the civilian population; and who caused it–Batista's forces, the July 26 Movement or other armed-opposition groups.

26. The government's embrace of Marxism and the practice of mobilizing young people to the countryside for various tasks brought about these fears. Although parental custody was never revoked, government policies gave the state a prominent role in the education of children and adolescents. After the U.S. government took the unprecedented step of allowing private citizens to give entry visa exemptions to children under 18, Operation *Pedro Pan* was born under the supervision of Monsignor Brian Walsh of the Catholic archdiocese in Miami. Approximately half the children and adolescents were immediately taken in by relatives; the other half remained under custody of the Catholic church. When the United States and Cuba agreed to the so-called Freedom Flights in 1965, most of the parents came to the United States and reunited with their children.

27. Most Cubans in exile live in the United States. In 2000, the U.S. census yielded the figure of 1,241,685 people of Cuban origin or ancestry. Towards the end of the 1990s, there were some 165,000 Cubans in other countries. In the early 1960s, the United States facilitated the entrance of Cubans, and in 1966 Congress passed the Cuban Adjustment Act. This act allowed those already in the United States and those who would arrive via the Freedom Flights (1965-1973) to apply for permanent residency. Cuban Adjustment and later regulations have thus made it easier for Cubans to acquire the much-coveted U.S. resi-

dency cards. The annual number of Cubans coming to the United States are as follows:

| | |
|---|---|
| 1959-1962 | 258,000 |
| 1965-1973 | 334,000 |
| 1980 | 125,000 |
| 1981-1990 | 122,000 |
| 1991-1999 | 159,000 |

Over more than four decades, rafters have been crossing the Florida Straits. Thousands of Cubans have set out to sea in the hope of reaching the United States. Without access to Cuban sources, it is impossible to determine the number of people who have died while trying to get out or during the journey. Estimates of casualties vary between 25 and 75 percent of those arriving safely. During the two main periods of illegal exits from Cuba–1959-1974 and 1983-1994, 61,840 Cubans entered the United States; accordingly, the number of lives lost would be between 15,460 and 46,380.

28. The phrase refers to the title of the document published in 1997 by the group known as *los cuatro* (see details in note 15). In 1957, the Catholic University Association published a report on the peasantry and the need for agrarian reform that conveyed the same idea (p.63 in *¿Por qué reforma agraria?*), in another context:

> It is time that our country cease being the private fiefdom of a few powerful interests. We hope that, in a few years, Cuba will not be the property of a few, but the true homeland of all Cubans.

29. Sustainable economic growth was never attained and, therefore, overall improvements in living standards never materialized.

30. The quote is Enrique Baloyra's (1942-1997) at a meeting held in 1996 about the Bay of Pigs invasion. Participants included former U.S. and Soviet government officials, Cuban opposition members, and scholars. Baloyra took part in both the anti-Batista and the anti-Castro struggles. At the time of his death, he was professor of political science and international relations at the University of Miami and a member of the Social Democratic Coordinating Committee. The volume edited by

James G. Blight and Peter Kornbluh, *Politics of Illusion: The Bay of Pigs Invasion Reexamined.* Boulder, CO: Lynne Rienner Publishers, 1998, published excerpts from the meeting's discussion; Baloyra's quote appears on pages 15-16.

31. A current example of a similar dilemma regards the embargo. The Cuban American National Foundation has effectively lobbied to prevent major changes in U.S. policy towards Cuba, even though important sectors of the foreign-policy establishment and Wall Street consider these beneficial to U.S. interests. CANF and most Cubans in Miami who support the embargo have resorted to U.S. means to do what they consider best for Cuba.

32. Carlos Rafael Rodríguez, a leading member of the pre-1959 Popular Socialist Party (Communist) and a prominent political figure from 1959 until the early 1990s, thus characterized the popular mood in the late 1960s; he used the phrase in an interview by Marifeli Pérez-Stable in 1984. Rodríguez died in 1998.

33. The microfaction drew mostly on members of the former PSP who opposed these policies–a second radicalization. They shared the critique that the Soviet Union and Latin American communist parties issued against Cuba in the late 1960s; most were purged and some imprisoned. Later, some old communists joined the human rights movement.

34. "The Era is Giving Birth to a Heart" was a popular song by Cuban folk singer Silvio Rodríguez. Its principal verse reads as follows:

> The era is giving birth to a heart
> It's exhausted, dying out of pain
> We have to rush
> Otherwise we won't have a future
> To a jungle anywhere in the world,
> In any street.

This song and others by Silvio at that time embodied the utopian illusions by revolutionary youths who became adults under the influence of the Cuban revolution and the New Left.

35. In 1988, the Cuban government invited a U.N. delegation for on-site observation of the human rights situation on the island. The CCPDH brought more than a thousand people to give testimony to this delegation; the group published a report in 1989 that later served as the basis for the United States and newly democratic governments in Czechoslovakia and Poland to sponsor the first resolution by the UN Human Rights Commission censuring the Cuban government in 1991.

36. In 1977, the United States and Cuba agreed to establish interests sections in their respective capitals; in diplomacy, these have an inferior rank to embassies. Since then, the interests sections have afforded the United States and Cuba direct channels of communication, albeit not normal diplomatic relations.

37. The Dialogue was the formula the Cuban government put into practice to announce the release of political prisoners and the authorization of family-reunification trips. These humanitarian measures had already been agreed upon with the Carter administration. Two meetings took place at the end of 1978; Havana used them as a means to "normalize" relations with what the government now called the "Cuban community abroad." The policy allowing Cubans abroad to visit Cuba perturbed the most radical sectors of Cuban society. They, after all, had cut off communication with their families and friends abroad as officially instructed and now, all of a sudden, they were asked to welcome them.

38. There have been exceptions to the emerging commitment to nonviolence. The following are two examples. In 1994, a six-member commando of the Party of National Democratic Unity (PUND) disembarked on a beach near the center of Cuba. One of the men, Humberto Real Suárez, killed a person and was condemned to death in a Cuban court; the sentence has yet to be carried out. The other five commandos each received 30-year prison terms. In 1997, bombs exploded in five hotels in Havana and at the restaurant *La Bodeguita del Medio.* The Cuban government arrested, tried, and condemned to death a Salvadoran man; his execution is still pending. The government accused him of working for CANF. Though he confessed to having placed the bombs, the man never said on whose behalf he did so. CANF denies having had anything to do with his actions.

39. Huber Matos–a Sierra Maestra *comandante* arrested and condemned to a 20-year jail term in late 1959 for opposing the radicalization outlined in this report–founded CID once he was freed in 1980. In the 1980s, CID had thousands of exile members in the United States and other countries and also sponsored *La Voz del CID*, a radio program broadcasted to Cuba.

40. On September 8, 1993, the bishops issued a milestone pastoral letter, "Love Hopes All Things"; Cubans commemorate their patron saint, the Virgin of Charity, on September 8. Among other subjects, the bishops emphasized "irritating policies" that should be ended: the closed and all-pervasive character of official ideology; limitations on freedom; excessive control by state security; the high number of people imprisoned for actions that should be decriminalized; and discrimination of citizens for their philosophical, political, and religious ideas. The bishops also called for a national dialogue that took into account the diversity in Cuban society. The pastoral letter updated the ideas of ENEC for the 1990s. The church today harbors a rich parish life, a network of social services, and multiple cultural and publishing endeavors. Thus far, however, it has not actively engaged in the defense of human rights. Many Catholics–priests, nuns, and laity–are critical of the church's inaction and would like to see it take a stronger, more effective ethical leadership in this regard.

41. Footnote 12 lists some political and economic proposals presented at that time that came to naught. During those years, the Center for the Study of the Americas (CEA) unofficially functioned as a seat for organic intellectuals committed to the renewal of Cuban socialism. CEA was, in effect, disbanded by the PCC in 1996. In 1994, the government removed the president of the University of Havana–a highly respected faculty member supported by his colleagues as well as by the local party cell–and put in his place a man more akin to party directives for tighter control over the university. In the cultural field, the Pablo Milanés Foundation, which sponsored autonomous cultural projects funded by Milanés' earnings as a singer and songwriter, was closed down. Between 1993 and 1996, the Magín group–an old Spanish word meaning imagination–was founded by women journalists seeking to sensitize Cuban media to gender issues.

42. In 2002, MROM proposed a Fundamental Charter of Rights and Duties for Cubans and opened 109 posts throughout the island where citizens could read the charter. At the end of 2002, more than 28,000 citizens had read the proposal and registered their opinions. The proposed charter has also been discussed by Cuban groups abroad who forwarded their opinions and comments to the MROM. The process of consultation ended on December 10, Human Rights Day. In February 2003, MROM started polling citizens to determine the charter's acceptance or rejection.

43. Rumors that ships from Florida were approaching to pick up those wishing to leave Cuba sparked the spontaneous demonstration. Once gathered, people did start to chant anti-government slogans and claims. Official sources cited 35 injured and 700 arrested. A couple of weeks earlier, the government had deliberately sunk the tugboat *13 de marzo*, causing 41 deaths, 10 of them minors.

44. Both polls were carried out by Bendixen & Associates at the request of the Cuban Study Group. Interviews were conducted with 800 Cuban residents in South Florida; the surveys have a three-to-five percent margin of error. Following the Elián González' case in 1999-2000, the Cuban Study Group was founded with the purpose of improving the much-battered image of the Cuban-American community. The group has been tracking Cuban South Florida's public opinion changes, already in progress by 1999 but overshadowed by the deep emotions stirred by the *balserito*'s arrival and departure.

45. Letter from the Reflection Roundtable of the Moderate Opposition to the Task Force on Memory, Truth, and Justice.

46. Military coups in Argentina and Uruguay had been preceded by the use of political violence by the *Montoneros*, *Tupamaros*, and other groups against their respective states. Their acts do not in any way justify or exculpate the subsequent military repression.

47. The self-amnesty law enacted by Pinochet contained, as only exceptions, those cases–such as Orlando Letelier's assassination in Washington–that jeopardized Chilean international relations. Once the dictatorship was over, democratic political forces thought it impossible to repeal the amnesty in order to initiate criminal proceedings.

Consequently, unveiling the truth–not the search for justice–became paramount. With the passage of time, the justice system has limited the effects of impunity by prosecuting some individuals for crimes committed during the dictatorship.

48. Torture was excluded from the commission's mandate.

49. The commission recommended the creation of reparation programs for the victims' families, and Aylwin's government immediately acted accordingly. By 1999, the Chilean state had paid $95 million in pensions, medical insurance policies, and scholarships.

50. Coordinated by military intelligence (DINA), the operation established a network of repression that took actions against the Pinochet opposition in the Southern Cone, Washington, and Rome.

51. The National party did not participate in these negotiations. The military vetoed Wilson Ferreira Aldunate, the party's exiled leader and, thus the *nacionales* abstained.

52. Though the amnesty did not cover political prisoners sentenced for homicide, many obtained their freedom nonetheless. Civilian courts reviewed these cases, and for those in which the military court's decision was ratified, the sentence was reduced three days per day served. The law thus ruled to compensate for the harshness of military sentences during the dictatorship.

53. Concerning reparations, the commission recommended granting $3,500 annually for six years to certain victims or their families. The government, however, announced a program of less than one thousand dollars to be awarded to fewer victims or their families than the commission recommended.

54. The truth commission's three members were: Belisario Betancur, former president of Colombia, Thomas Buergenthal, former president of the Inter-American Court of Human Rights and law professor at George Washington University, and Reinaldo Figueredo, former foreign minister of Venezuela. The *ad hoc* commission was made up of Salvadorans Abraham Rodríguez, Reynaldo Galindo Pohl, and Eduardo Molina Olivares.

55. The U.S. Congress passed FOIA in 1967; it was amended in 1975 to give the citizenry access to federal government information. A process was established to request the information in writing and certain regulations to fulfil these requests were put in place.

56. In Czechoslovakia, Václav Havel opposed these laws.

57. Don Jaime Castillo, then president of the Human Rights Commission of Chile and founder of the Latin American Secretariat of Human Rights (SELADEH) thus characterized the situation: "Those who are blind in their left eye, and those who are blind in their right eye."

58. International law considers crimes against humanity certain serious offenses committed as part of a systematic or widespread pattern of behavior. A democratic Cuba could use the listings of crimes against humanity by the Rome Statute (1998), which established the International Court of Justice, to determine whether or not these actually occurred in Cuba. "Crimes against humanity" are any of the following acts when committed as part of a widespread or systematic attack directed against any civilian population, with knowledge of the attack: (a) murder; (b) extermination; (c) enslavement; (d) deportation or forcible transfer of population; (e) imprisonment or other severe deprivation of physical liberty in violation of fundamental rules of international law; (f) torture; (g) rape, sexual slavery, enforced prostitution, forced pregnancy, enforced sterilization, or any other form of sexual violence of comparable gravity; (h) persecution against any identifiable group or collectivity on political, racial, national, ethnic, cultural, religious, or gender; (i) enforced disappearance of persons; (j) the crime of apartheid; (k) other inhumane acts of a similar character intentionally causing great suffering, or serious injury to body or to mental or physical health. Though not retroactive, the statute codifies international criteria and rules concerning crimes against humanity as well as war crimes that have been in process since the 1940s. Crimes against humanity entail an obligation to investigate, prosecute, and punish criminals, without the benefits of pardons or amnesties.

59. A noteworthy event–a consequence of the poor conditions in Cuban prisons–was the death of Pedro Luis Boitel on May 25, 1972, after a 53-day hunger strike. Boitel opposed Batista and later the revolutionary

government's radical turn. After strong official pressures, Boitel lost the election for president of the University Student Federation in 1959 by a slight margin. The winner was Rolando Cubelas, a man then trusted by the top leadership, who subsequently participated in an attempt against Fidel Castro's life. Boitel was arrested and sentenced to a 10-year term; additional charges were pressed against him once in prison. Boitel had often resorted to hunger strikes in protest for the treatment he received.

60. During a conference held in Cuba in March 2001 on the 40th anniversary of *Playa Girón*/Bay of Pigs, former interior minister Ramiro Valdés acknowledged that, just during the weekend before the invasion, approximately 20,000 people were arrested.

61. For example, after three years in jail, Dr. Oscar Elías Biscet was released on October 31, 2002. On December 6, he was arrested again as he tried to enter a house in Lawton, a Havana neighborhood, to participate in a forum on human rights; the police also arrested eleven others. As of March 2003, Biscet remained in jail and, as in his prior arrest, is considered a prisoner of conscience. The life of Martin Luther King, Jr. was an inspiration in his becoming a human rights activist in Cuba.

62. The Geneva conventions and protocols could serve as the basis for an international investigation of how the wars in Angola and Ethiopia were conducted by all sides.

63. Valdés again served as interior minister between 1980 and 1985.

64. Between 1963 and 1967, the Interior Ministry tried to enforce a rehabilitation plan whereby political prisoners were forced to attend Marxism classes and accept other political conditions. The term *plantado* arose then to describe the overwhelming majority of political prisoners who refused to join the so-called rehabilitation. Del Valle's progressive plan did not entail political rehabilitation.

65. The *plantado* prisoner Mario Chanes de Armas served a 30-year sentence, almost certainly the longest sentence for political reasons meted in the 20th century. He participated in the assault of Moncada Barracks (1953), the *Granma* expedition (1956), and in the July 26 Movement against Batista. During that dictatorship, he served almost two years in prison.

66. Carlos Rafael Rodríguez, "Cuatro años de reforma agraria," *Cuba Socialista* (May 1963), pp. 12 and 14. Rodríguez belonged to the Popular Socialist Party (communist) before 1959, and was a high-ranking official until a few years before he died in 1998. When he wrote the cited article, he was president of the National Institute for Agrarian Reform (INRA).

67. *Granma*, April 14, 1966.

68. José Luis Hernández, one of the prisoners in the tractor trailer and a participant in the conference, asked Osmany Cienfuegos about the incident; members of Brigade 2506 identified Cienfuegos as the person who ordered the unventilated vehicle locked. Cienfuegos denied having given the order, but admitted his responsibility in the matter since, as public works minister, he had jurisdiction over the tractor trailer.

69. The claim's full text can be found in www.granma.cubaweb.cu/. In addition, the Cuban government filed suit against the United States for economic damages, actions that do not fall within the bounds of *Cuban National Reconciliation.*

70. In 1968, Orlando Bosch was convicted to a 10-year sentence for attacking a Polish merchant ship in Florida; he served four years before being released on parole. In 1976 he was arrested by Venezuelan authorities for the explosion of the *Cubana de Aviación* flight from Barbados. He was prosecuted and convicted; he was acquitted on appeal. In 1988 he returned to the United States and was immediately arrested for having violated his parole in the Polish ship case. Contrary to the advice by the Immigration and Naturalization Service and the Justice Department, President George H. W. Bush set him free, after a campaign in his favor by sectors of the exile community.

In 1983, Eduardo Arocena was arrested, and he was brought to trial in New York a year later, charged with conspiracy, with the murder of Félix García Rodríguez (a Cuban diplomat at the United Nations), and with perjury. He was given life imprisonment and must serve 20-40 years before being eligible for parole.

Five Cubans exiles were involved in the assassination of Orlando Letelier in Washington. Three were arrested, prosecuted, and convicted for perjury. José Dionisio Suárez and Virgilio Paz were missing for twelve years. Once captured, they were prosecuted for conspiracy and murder, and sentenced to twelve years. After serving seven, the Immigration and Naturalization Service took charge of them and released them in 2001.

In many cases of terrorism in Miami and other Cuban communities, those responsible have not been identified nor punished. In the future, as many of these cases as possible should be elucidated. It should also be determined whether Cuban intelligence had a hand in planning and implementing some of them.

71. Ramón Saúl Sánchez is the person cited. He was released in 1986. In 1995, Sánchez founded *Movimiento Democracia* based on the principles of nonviolence and civic resistance.

72. See two reports on Miami: Americas Watch, *Dangerous Dialogue: Attacks on Freedom of Expression in Miami's Cuban Exile Community* (1992) and Human Rights Watch, *Dangerous Dialogue Revisited: Threats to Freedom of Expression in Miami's Cuban Exile Community* (1994). Currently, representatives of Cuban Miami are part of the "Celebrate Free Speech" project sponsored by People for the American Way Foundation–a liberal group–to improve relations among different groups of Miami with a history of confrontations.

73. Domingo Moreira, "Project Varela Leads Cuba to Freedom," *The Miami Herald*, June 5, 2002.

74. José J. Basulto, "Ayudemos al pueblo cubano," *El Nuevo Herald*, November 11, 2001.

75. Jorge Más Santos, "Entre cubanos está la solución," *El Nuevo Herald* (February 2, 2003).

76. See, for example, the National Security Archive's www.gwu.edu/~nsarchiv/ for relevant documents declassified by virtue of the Freedom of Information Act.

77. In planning and executing these attempts, the CIA worked with the mafia, the opposition in Cuba, and with its own people. In 1975, the Cuban leader gave then Senator George McGovern a list of 24 attempts on his life, allegedly CIA-inspired. Church found no evidence of CIA involvement in these cases. The Cuban government suit alleges a total of 637 attempts.

78. *Alleged Assassination Plots Involving Foreign Leaders.* New York: W.W. Norton & Company, Inc., 1976, p. XIX. After September 11, Church's warnings have again become relevant as the proscription against assassination was waived by President Bush in 2001 in order to ease the U.S. fight against terrorism. Many such measures taken by the administration have been strongly criticized in the United States and abroad.

79. Letter to the Task Force on Memory, Truth, and Justice.

80. Letter from the Reflection Roundtable of the Moderate Opposition to the Task Force on Memory, Truth, and Justice.

81. "Algo se mueve en Cuba: En camino hacia la madurez cívica," *Revista Vitral.* November-December 2002. www.vitral.org

## Additional or Dissenting Comments

I would like to share with readers some valuable lessons I learned during the two years of work with the Task Force on Memory, Truth, and Justice. Let me make a confession outright: when I joined the group, I not only did not know much about Cuban history, but I also harbored an unfounded prejudice against Cuban exiles.

Since then, I have garnered valuable information regarding the real motives impelling the overwhelming majority of Cubans to oppose Batista's dictatorship. Without doubt, my most valuable lesson had to do with the many and diverse groups who courageously confronted that dictator. Some members of the task force, now in exile, spent long years in jail for opposing the new dictatorship imposed after the revolution's triumph. Due to my ignorance, I was surprised to learn that these same people had fought against Batista, having shared the same ideals of freedom and social justice held by most Cubans during the 1950s. Only the authoritarian imposition by one of the groups that had participated in the revolution over the others explains why these people who also fought for freedom would end up being so harshly punished.

This newfound understanding has made me think a lot about possible parallels with the Spanish case. What if the *republicanos* (loyalists to the Second Republic) had won the civil war? Could it not have been the case—in view of the different political projects that coexisted within the Republican side—that one of them, in particular the Communist faction, might have been tempted to exclude the others? In fact, Communist reprisals against other sectors within the Republican coalition had already started during the war. Had the conflict ended in favor of the Republic, we could have easily witnessed the imprisonment and exile of moderate Republicans, Socialists, and Anarchists shortly thereafter. In fact, some Spanish Communists ended up contributing to the Soviet turn that the Cuban revolution took in 1959. This comparison allows a better understanding of the rich diversity within the Cuban opposition on the island and in exile: a good many of them paid dearly for upholding their democratic ideals, albeit not all opposition groups were equally committed to democracy.

The task force also gave me the opportunity to learn about the cruel, repressive tactics of a dictatorship that–brandishing an alleged defense of egalitarian ideals—has silenced, or tried to silence all discordant opinions, trampling some of the most basic citizen rights. The reports of prestigious international organizations (Amnesty International, Human Rights

Watch, *Reporteros sin Fronteras*, etc.) and the testimonials I heard from members of the task force were particularly enlightening.

I have surely learned a lot from those who oppose Fidel Castro's dictatorship, both in exile and on the island. As I have already indicated, the former have shown me their rich diversity and the preponderance among them of democratic ideals. The latter—especially Oswaldo Payá whom I was lucky to meet in person—have given me an encouraging message: that for years Cuban civil society has been trying to rebuild and articulate an alternative political project, based on regaining freedom of election, association, opinion, etc., and an unyielding commitment to nonviolence. I was also gratified to learn that most Cubans hope democracy does not entail an increase of socioeconomic inequalities among them, even as elections will determine the ideological direction of future democratic governments.

I truly hope this report has an impact commensurate to the expectations and good will with which the task force crafted it. Above all, I hope it helps to establish an open dialogue among all Cubans who support a democratic Cuba. If guided by tolerance and a desire to seek liberties, the mere exchange of opinions would likely reveal to Cubans much greater consensus than they can now imagine. That is what happened to the *antifranquistas* who met in Munich in 1962: initial suspicions notwithstanding, those in exile and those who lived in Spain quickly discovered that what they had in common, a democratic political project, carried more weight than their differences, which enabled them to work jointly on a common platform of democratization. May this report contribute to a Cuban reunion with similar results.

Let's hope that Castro's dictatorship, as well as all other dictatorships, accept free elections and an unconditional respect for human rights as the only legitimate form of government.

Last, I would like to express my sincerest appreciation to the steering committee, particularly to Marifeli Pérez-Stable, for having invited me to join the task force. I obviously learned a lot from our meetings. Prejudices collapse when there is a flow of information (thus, the importance of unveiling the truth of what actually happened) and when there is an open and rich dialogue (thus, the imperative of a reunion among all Cubans). May this report also help dissipate the doubts still existing among the democratic left worldwide regarding condemnation of the Castro regime, and may it also generate a new understanding of the reasons that led so many Cubans into exile.

***Paloma Aguilar Fernández***

Even though a democratic Cuba is not yet in the offing, sooner or later it will be. As a Dominican, I was brought up under the formidable influence and promise of the Cuban revolution. Moreover, thousands of U.S. marines invaded the Dominican Republic in 1965 under the pretense of preventing a "second Cuba." Witnessing my country's occupation by foreign troops left an indelible mark on my political development: for many years after the invasion, I stood up for the ideals of the Cuban revolution.

However, my work in the human rights field from the mid-1970s onward led me to embrace the full breadth of democratic values that today underpin my political convictions.

I staunchly defend the ideals of freedom, justice, and equality; I also believe in the indivisibility of all rights–civil, political, economic, social, and cultural. Their joint pursuit and the search for individual happiness are possible only under a democratic system of government, one that supports and encourages the free flow of ideas, multiple political parties, and democratic succession.

The Cuban people live under a severe, one-party dictatorship whose political leadership is kept in power by the force of arms, not ballots. Castro's regime has become a reality that–even as a utopia–is patently anachronistic. Even though it seems impenetrable, I am convinced that from within Cuba itself a sociopolitical movement will emerge to make the regime collapse.

In the transition to a democratic system of government based on full political equality, the Cuban people and their future leaders will have to make difficult decisions in relation to a past of human rights violations incurred by the current government, in power for 44 years thus far.

There is no single road towards recovering memory, finding the truth, providing justice, and searching for reconciliation; the Cuban people will have to build their own destiny in that regard. Notwithstanding, the reflection in *Cuban National Reconciliation* could be useful for that day, which will come sooner or later. There is, however, one fact worth underlining: the principles and standards for protecting human rights and punishing their violation are now universal and, therefore, transcend national boundaries.

In Cuba, as in every country of the world, may ethics triumph!

***Roberto Álvarez***

*Cuban National Reconciliation* is a promising and encouraging report. Through its work, the task force has helped establish that a *better future is possible* for Cuba. We did not ask for nor did we wait for anyone's permission to dialogue. The report is perforce insufficient, and its content does not fully represent the preferences of each participant, which is why it is an invitation for others to continue thinking about reconciliation.

The Cuban opposition often espouses the idea of reconciliation without fruitful results: its ranks are divided by the lack of a constructive reply from those to whom they are reaching out. The Cuban regime shares a culture of intransigence and intolerance with certain sectors of the exile community. The much-touted meetings held occasionally in Havana between government officials and Cuban exiles never had–from the government's perspective–reconciliation as an objective, but the accomplishment of certain pressing political objectives. Thus, one may say there are intransigent sectors brandishing different agendas but sharing a political culture that considers dialogue and reconciliation tantamount to treason. Within this common perspective, reconciliation is worse than surrender; it is simply switching sides. That is still the ethical and political landscape of a nation marred by the schism of two civil wars (in the 1950s and in the 1960s) and torn between a permanent diaspora–a majority of whom were exiled and banished–and Cubans on the island.

National reconciliation is a spiritual and political imperative: the best guarantee for Cuba's future stability and the definitive ethical healing of a political culture of violence. Only a few on one side or the other of the barricades are bent on raising obstacles to its realization. We must *think* about national reconciliation and initiate a dialogue–without awaiting permissions or intermediaries–at all levels of Cuban society. A dialogue is not a public relations *show* orchestrated by one of the parties.

For a process of reconciliation to be successful, certain conditions should be met, though not necessarily simultaneously. The following are especially noteworthy.

- Reclaiming the *moral and political autonomy* of all those who, even today, are propelled by a few–in Havana or in exile—to perpetrate new violations and abuses that compromise their personal integrity. No authority has the right to impose an alleged *due obedience* to immoral orders or actions. No one has the right to taint our integrity by making us act against our conscience, nor should we allow them to do so.

- Promoting a *genuine dialogue* aimed at attaining a *pluralistic understanding*–which does not translate into *approval*–of the past and a commitment to overcome its polarization. Such a dialogue would only be worthy of the name if *old enemies* convene as *political adversaries*, both showing a disposition to reconsider the means used in their confrontation and, together, to explore possible compromises for a peaceful resolution.

- Crafting and consolidating a *new political culture* based on tolerance, pluralism, democratic dialogue for peaceful conflict resolution, and full respect for the exercise of freedoms as well as individual and collective rights. Abolishing the death penalty is a priority that cannot be postponed.

- Overcoming the current paradigm for development based on state socialism: the permanent uprooting of a culture of intolerance that has sanctioned *political violence* requires no less, in my judgment, and thus I offer it as a fourth basic condition for a true dialogue. We need a paradigm capable of conciliating representative democracy with participatory democracy, environmental protection with the needs of the economy, private enterprise with the safeguard of social, economic, and cultural rights, and majority will with respect for minorities. We need not only to eradicate *political violence*, but to forge a new social pact capable of purging Cuban society of *structural violence.*

Reconciliation is, therefore, an *essential tool* to advance towards the final objective: a new political culture born out of a new paradigm of sustainable human development.

***Juan Antonio Blanco Gil***

*Cuban National Reconciliation* gave a group of Cubans, along with some excellent colleagues of other nationalities, the opportunity to dialogue and rethink the roots of our national problem and, above all, to think about how true national reconciliation could help us heal the many wounds opened throughout all these years.

Both in Cuba and in exile, the use of violence and terrorism has been rooted in the absence of a true national dialogue throughout our history and in the violent ways we have confronted our political crises.

Saddest of all is the fact that both winners and losers have tended to justify the use of violence and indiscriminate terrorism. Even today there are Cubans on both sides who still justify their actions, without giving a moment's thought to the cost paid in lives by both sides and, even worse, to the innocent victims and the dismal consequences for the Cuban nation.

Those of us who in the past–in one way or another–took active part in the violence cannot morally continue justifying our actions based on the genuineness of our ideals. The very actions we carried out against the physical integrity of other human beings taint these ideals. The end can never justify the means. Neither can state terrorism be morally justified by the uncompromising defense of revolutionary ideals. For a long time, many of us have been both victims and oppressors, depending on the circumstances or on the lens through which we look at history.

For some, true peace among Cubans will only be reached when we sit down together–without resentment or desire for revenge but without forgetting the past–and admit the duality we have maintained: as the oppressors we might have once been, let us ask forgiveness from our victims; as the victims we might also have been, let us be willing to forgive our oppressors. Such an act of reconciliation, inspired by love for our fellow Cubans, would set an example for future generations and offer them an incentive to avoid making the same mistakes. Only then will we live peacefully in a more just, free, prosperous, and fraternal Cuba.

Only two issues were not discussed in the meetings of the Task Force on Memory, Truth, and Justice due to lack of consensus among members: the embargo and confiscated properties. Regarding the embargo, I do want to note that, in spite of the group's differences, there is an international consensus classifying "unilateral coercive measures" as violations of human rights, duly expressed in resolutions by the United Nations Human Rights Commission and the General Assembly. The Cuban government uses the unilateral U.S. embargo to justify totally unrelated internal situations. The burden of this unjust policy, however, has been borne by the Cuban people.

*Siro del Castillo*

Reconciliation among Cubans, on the island and off, is key to the future of Cuba, as this report so eloquently argues. The process of reconciliation has already begun. Reconciliation in families has advanced significantly; the warlike rhetoric on both sides of the Florida Straits has decreased somewhat. In Miami, reconciliation in the Cuban and Cuban-American community has begun, as those with differing views about the island learn to debate their views, rather than seek to impose them by force.

But political reconciliation between the exile community and the island remains a distant hope. This report argues persuasively that genuine reconciliation will require the creation of a culture, in Cuba and in its diaspora, that is more tolerant of differences, and more committed to pluralism than the culture that exists today. The report also argues that a democratic and pluralistic Cuba must confront its past, and the history of human rights violations that has marked Cuba, especially during the sixties.

I agree that Cuba must confront its past, and I think the report makes a useful contribution in its acknowledgement that there are human rights violations on all sides –on the side of the Cuban government and on the side of its opponents –that must be addressed. Evaluation of these abuses must be viewed against a larger context, not to justify, but to understand more deeply the social and political forces at work. The tactics employed by Castro must be seen against a backdrop of unmitigated hostility from Washington that Cuban officials felt threatened the government's very existence. The tragedy of September 11 brought about the extraordinary security measures by the administration of George W. Bush that many believe are eroding the core civil liberties that define the essence of America democracy. Appeals to external threats should never be used to justify curbing basic freedoms, whether in the United States or in Cuba.

Because Cuba is unlikely to experience a fundamental change of government in the near future, even in a post-Castro era, at this point the likelihood is low that Cuba will confront its past in the near term through a truth commission, or some similar approach. But that does not mean that the process of reconciliation cannot advance. This report should not be read to mean that Cubans abroad should not be in dialogue with the Cuban government, holding out a full reckoning with the past as a pre-condition for contact.

I think it important to encourage discussion and dialogue between the Cuban exile and Cuban-American community, on the one side, and Cubans on the island and the Cuban government, on the other. The creation of a more pluralistic and more tolerant culture is a process, a process that should be encouraged through dialogue and exchange of opinions.

*Joe Eldridge*

As the report indicates, those of us who have signed it do not necessarily agree with every phrasing or even every particular comment. What I particularly do support, however, is the moderate, conciliatory, self-critical tone, which Cubans on both sides of the Florida Straits will have to adopt to achieve true national reconciliation, something that would be of immense benefit to all parties concerned, including the United States.

I think that some particular past U.S. policies could be defended, and the report does not have it, but that may simply reflect my own political and national bias; I was one of the few U.S. participants with no Cuban roots to be involved in the project. In any case, since I deal with U.S.-Cuban relations extensively in my forthcoming book, I do not believe my own views will be misunderstood.

Although I am not opposed to the death penalty, in principle, for high treason or certain crimes of violence, I would feel uncomfortable advocating it in Cuba under the present circumstances. In a democratic Cuba, I would leave the decision up to an elected government and would respect whatever decision it reached on the matter.

*Mark Falcoff*

As a group, we were able to dialogue and produce a report that brought together people of different positions. Unfortunately, we did not have members who currently live in Cuba due to the restrictions the Cuban government imposes for participating in forums like ours. This limits the expression of the authentic and diverse viewpoints that exist in Cuba today regarding the issues we discussed. In my particular case, I live abroad due to the arbitrary decision made to deny me entry to my own country. Until the late 1990s, I was a party member and, thus, my experience was much different from other members of the task force. These differences were, I believe, constructive for the dialogue we were able to sustain.

The only way to overcome the problems Cuba faces today is by acknowledging them, presenting options, and developing the participatory capacity of all Cubans as regards the country's destiny. As *Cuban National Reconciliation* so eloquently states, these tasks are primarily a responsibility of Cubans living on the island. Cubans there are not represented by the official, conservative elite that, from the seat of power, pretends to speak for all Cubans; nor are they represented by the different opposition groups that have emerged in response to the politics of silence the government has imposed. Cubans on the island need to speak outside the official and manipulated farces the government stages today. I am certain of one thing: among growing sectors of the population, there is a will to change that cannot be ignored.

In view of the widespread fear Cubans have of expressing their opinions or of losing the modest positions they have acquired that ease their daily lives, it is difficult to predict what is going to happen there. That is the reason why the incentive for dialogue, reflection, and reconciliation is so necessary today.

It is imperative we open a genuine, participatory process that brings together representatives from all sectors and that allows all Cubans a voice and a vote, on the island and abroad, no matter what their views: real contradictions are necessary. The task force marks a first effort in the right direction: without aspirations for power or hegemony, the report seeks only to start an unavoidable process regarding the history and memories that divide us; we should discuss it in the light of much-needed national integration and reconciliation. Though many today are still reluctant to do so, we must acknowledge there are many Cubans–on the island and abroad–with values and principles, just as there are opportunists on both sides. The ways and objectives we pursue define our values–neither side has an *a priori* claim on values.

As *Cuban National Reconciliation* argues, the Cuban government has committed violations of human rights, and the opposition in the sixties perpetrated abuses. However, when stating that the principal responsibility for these abuses lies with the Cuban government (on the grounds governments have more resources at their disposal), the support that the U.S. government gave to some opposition sectors at the time, as well as U.S. policies of permanent pressure and aggression against Cuba should not be ignored. The U.S. government is also responsible for what happened. The issues at hand were not exclusively Cuban problems.

Last, I would like to ratify my position regarding the Revolution, which was widely popular in the 1960s for its great accomplishments in defending social justice and empowering majority sectors of Cuban society. The loss of popularity has been a gradual process in view of the increasing imposition of authoritarianism, repression, and lack of options.

***Fernando González Rey***

Participating in the task force was worthwhile. We had substantive discussions and offer as legacy an intelligent document that will certainly point the debate in the right direction once the moment of transition comes. In general, the task proposed by the group that gathered around *Cuban National Reconciliation* is impossible to carry out at this time. A reconciliation of any kind implies an acceptance of guilt, regret, and tolerance regarding the criteria and attitudes. That is the case when lovers, sports teams, hostile countries, or opposing social segments reconcile, and it is also the case with Cubans. For reconciliation, as for dancing the tango, it takes two. Unfortunately, in this case, there is and there will always be only one party: the democratic opposition. The Castro regime simply does not step forward in this sense and will, in fact, duly dismiss this report as a U.S.-inspired maneuver to destabilize it.

Why is the Castro regime not capable of acknowledging mistakes, crimes, or abuses? Why are its adversaries always worms, annexationists, terrorists, CIA agents, or greedy twerps on imperialism's payroll? These beliefs and positions constitute the essence of Castroism: a group with a discourse based on unquestionable certainties, rooted in delirious readings of history, messianic interpretations of the role of the leading elite, and undisputable forecasts about their destiny. That is, we are in the presence of men who own the past, the present, and the future. They claim to be the direct descendants of 19th century Cuban independence fighters, who–after a shameful and compromised republican interval–have installed themselves permanently in power to save Cuban society from always voracious U.S. imperialism and from the submissiveness of some bad Cubans. For their epic poem, they need the people united without cleavages, following the leader and his sacred word, which is studied at work and schools as if it were the scriptures of a unanimous sect committed to the oral transmission of the tribe's traditions.

The Castro regime's incapacity to dialogue or change was clearly evident (again and again) during the Book Fair in Guadalajara at the end of 2002, when what could have been a rich exchange of opinions turned out to be a pogrom against Rafael Rojas and other intellectuals linked to the Mexican magazine *Letras Libres.* Castroism wanted to conquer, not convince; it had no interest in discussing, rather in insulting, silencing, and crushing the other. Of course, what else could be done with worms who want the nation's destruction?

The position of the Castro regime is clearly understood. A regime founded on the type of nonsense and arbitrariness that serve as bases for its false legitimacy, could not–by its very essence–open itself to debate without collapsing. This realization leads us to discover the paradox of *Cuban National Reconciliation*: if the Castro regime were to grant the other his humanity and accept his reasons as valid, if it were to harbor a single doubt about its own arguments or recognize all historical interpretations to be partial or relative in nature, at that moment it would irreversibly fall apart. As a self-contained, hermetic verbal construction, its discourse does not allow amendments or rectifications. Certain, deep, and eternal hate is a propitious environment for the Castro regime. How can it reconcile when it would disintegrate the very instant it assumes the humble attitude–intellectual and human–that reconciliation requires?

**Carlos Alberto Montaner**

In this long struggle, I have lived through discouraging and frustrating moments as I realized how difficult it was to find the right strategy and the proper tactics against the rigidity of an absolute system such as Cuba's. However, no effort has been in vain, and ours found organizations and people that share our passion for *la patria* (the nation). I buried all desire for revenge and "an eye for an eye and a tooth for a tooth" long ago. I understood a nation could not be built on hate and revenge, but through understanding, tolerance, and love, as well as truth and justice. That is why, when Marifeli honored me with the invitation to join the task force, I did not hesitate in accepting, even when I knew I would find myself surrounded by intellectuals, scholars, and professionals who had little to do with my world of trade unions. However, we started out with a shared theme: memory, truth, and justice as a silver bridge for national reconciliation.

It was a challenge that would test our experience and maturity. It is difficult for Cubans to understand that our truths are not absolute and that there are other truths that we should consider in order to make a fair analysis of our history and reality. I think we mostly accomplished our goals, cognizant of the fact that striving for perfection often prevents achieving what is good. We did a lot, probably more than we initially expected. At the three meetings–in plenary sessions and working groups–held over two years, we learned to listen to one another, to reflect, and to formulate the criteria set forth in this report.

The support of qualified specialists from other countries was a great boon to our objectives, that is, preparing useful tools for Cuba's present and future as this report purports to be. I agree with the observation that reconciliation has, in effect, already started, and we should learn from the experiences of other countries in finding our own peace.

I will not make any specific comments on the report's different sections. However, I do want to underscore the contributions made by different social actors within Cuba, which notably enrich the report. *Cuban National Reconciliation*, indeed, also opened a space for those without a voice. Everyone–in Cuba and abroad–should know about the positions of those prevented from freely accessing the world of ideas in the "information age."

Last, I would like to acknowledge the excellent guidance we received during the work of the task force, led by Marifeli Pérez-Stable's creative genius, supported by the professors Jorge Domínguez's and Pedro Freyre's brilliance and management skills, and assisted by an efficient administrative team. Time will issue the final verdict on this project, which is an appeal to the hearts and minds of our compatriots. We wager on success.

**Pedro Pérez Castro**

## Biographical Notes

**Paloma Aguilar Fernández** received her Ph.D. in political science and sociology in 1995. Since then, she has been a professor in the Department of Political Science at UNED (Madrid). She has also taught as a Tinker Professor at the University of Wisconsin-Madison. Her publications include *Memoria y olvido de la guerra civil española* (Alianza Editorial, 1996); the English version was issued by Berghahn Books, New York and Oxford, and is entitled *Memory and Amnesia. The Role of the Spanish Civil War in the Transition to Democracy.*

**Roberto Álvarez** is a Dominican attorney and businessman. He is a former diplomat and has served as a human rights and legal official for the Organization of American States, and as a consultant for the Inter-American Development Bank (IDB), the United Nations Latin American Institute for the Prevention of Crime and the Treatment of Offenders (ILANUD), and Amnesty International. He has taught at several universities. He writes about human rights and international relations for U.S. and Dominican newspapers and magazines.

**Juan Antonio Blanco Gil** (Havana, 1947) taught philosophy at the University of Havana, and the history of international relations at the *Instituto Superior de Relaciones Internacionales* (ISRI). He was also a diplomat and a foreign policy analyst for the Foreign Ministry and the Central Committee of the Communist Party of Cuba (1972-1992). He founded and directed the Félix Varela Center in Havana (1993-1997). At present he lives in Canada, and since 1998 has been the director of International Cooperation for *Human Rights Internet.*

**Siro del Castillo** (Havana, 1943), a former political prisoner, has worked to assist refugees in the United States–from Cuba and other countries–and to defend human rights in the Caribbean. His record of civic activism is extensive. In 2000 he received two prestigious awards. In February, the Florida Immigrant Advocacy Center awarded him the Justice and Freedom for All Award, and in September Facts About Cuban Exiles (FACE) selected him for the Directors' Award for his services to the community.

**Elisa Vilano Chovel** was born in Guanabacoa, Cuba and arrived in the United States more than 40 years ago as one of the 14,000 children of the Operation Pedro Pan. At age 21, she became a widow: her husband, US Army Aviation captain, Thomas F. Flanigan, died in Vietnam. She has three children and four grandchildren. She is founder and chair of the board of Operation Pedro Pan Group, Inc., an organization serving today's needy children. She is a top sales realtor with Esslinger-Wooten-Maxwell in Miami.

**Jorge I. Domínguez** is a professor of political science at Harvard University. His books include *Cuba: Order and Revolution* and *To Make A World Safe for Revolution: Cuba's Foreign Policy.* He served as president of the Institute of Cuban Studies from 1990 to 1994.

**María Domínguez** is an attorney and a professor in Miami. She is the founder and director of the Human Rights Institute of Saint Thomas University. Under her leadership the institute has received wide recognition, including the ARETE 2001 Prize ("arete" is the Greek term for virtue) for the Program of the Year, given by the Ethics and Certification Commission of Miami-Dade County.

**Joseph T. Eldridge** is university chaplain and adjunct faculty for the School of International Service at American University. Until assuming the position of university chaplain in 1997, Reverend Eldridge spent more than twenty years working in the public policy arena as an advocate and analyst of international human rights and humanitarian issues. In 1974 he co-founded the Washington Office on Latin America, a public policy and human rights organization, and served as its director for twelve years. He lived in Santiago, Chile from 1970-1973 where he worked for an agency of the United Methodist Church.

**Mark Falcoff** is a resident scholar at the American Enterprise Institute. He received his Ph.D. from Princeton University and has taught at the Universities of Illinois, Oregon, and California (Los Angeles). His books include *Small Countries, Large Issues; Modern Chile, 1970-89: A Critical History;* and *A Culture of Its Own: Taking Latin America Seriously.* His new book, *Cuba the Morning After: Normalization and its Discontents,* will be published in mid-2003.

**Damián Fernández** (Pinar del Río, Cuba, 1957) teaches international relations at Florida International University. He specializes in Cuban politics and Latin American foreign relations. His books include *Cuba* *and the Politics of Passion* and *Cuba, The Elusive Nation: Reinterpretations of National Identity* (co-edited with Madeline Cámara).

**Lino B. Fernández** (Esmeralda, Camagüey, Cuba, 1931) is a psychiatrist. He is married to Emilia Luzárraga and has three children and eight grandchildren. He was a political prisoner in Cuba from February 1961 to November 1977. In 1959 he helped found the *Movimiento de Recuperación Revolucionaria* in Havana. In 1990, he was a co-founder of the *Coordinadora Social Demócrata* in Miami.

**Pedro A. Freyre** (Havana, 1949) is an attorney. He graduated from Belén High School (Miami, 1967) and from the University of Miami (B.A., 1970; School of Law, 1975). He is a member of the board of birectors of the Florida Humanities Council and the Florida Immigrant Advocacy Center, and is also vicepresident of the Miami-Dade Community Relations Board. He was an adjunct political science instructor at Florida International University (1988-1995). In January 2003, Morehouse College (Atlanta, Georgia) gave him the Gandhi-King-Ikeda Award, in recognition of his work for peace and justice.

**Carlos García-Vélez** (Havana, 1934) is the grandson of Calixto García Íñiguez, a general in the Liberation Army, and of Vicente Martínez Ybor, the founder of Ybor City in Tampa, Florida. Until 1960 he was a lawyer in Cuba. Since then he has lived in Miami. For 30 years he worked for the AMERIFIRST Bank, where he began his career as a teller and ended as the president. He currently serves on the board of directors of several insurance companies. He is a U.S. citizen.

**Fernando Luis González Rey** (Havana, 1949) has a Ph.D. in psychology. At the University of Havana, he served as professor, dean of the School of Psychology (1987-1990), and vice-provost of the University (1990-1995). He participated in the literacy campaign in the early days of the revolution, and was an active member of the Young Communists and the Communist Party. In 1995, during his absence, he was expelled from the party. He now lives in Brazil and is a professor at several universities.

**Carl-Johan Groth**, a retired ambassador, served as the head of mission at the Swedish embassies in Havana and Santiago de Chile in the first half of the 1970s. From 1983 to 1986, he headed the Swedish delegation to the annual meetings in Geneva of the UN Commission on Human Rights. In 1991, he participated in a UN exploratory mission on human rights to El Salvador. In 1992, Ambassador Groth was appointed the UN Special Rapporteur on the Situation of Human Rights in Cuba; the mandate was terminated at the March 1998 session of the Human Rights Commission.

**Juan Ernesto Méndez** is a professor of law at the University of Notre Dame. Since 2000 he has been a member of the Inter-American Commission on Human Rights, which he will chair until 2003. He served as director of the Inter-American Institute of Human Rights between 1996 and 1999, as well as executive director of the Americas Division, and as general counsel of Human Rights Watch between 1982 and 1996. He was a political prisoner in Argentina from 1975 to 1977.

**Carlos Alberto Montaner** (Havana, 1943) has been a professor in Puerto Rico and a visiting professor at universities in Ecuador, Guatemala, and Peru. He is the author of many books. His latest books about Cuba include *Viaje al corazón de Cuba: Un siglo de doloroso aprendizaje*. He publishes a weekly column in several Spanish, U.S., and Latin American newspapers. He has lived in Madrid since 1970.

**Eusebio Mujal-León** is a professor and former chair of the Department of Government at Georgetown University. A specialist in Western European and Latin American politics, he has written numerous articles and is the author and editor of several books. He has recently published "Charismatic Post-Totalitarianism—The Castro Regime in Comparative Perspective" in *Problems of Post-Communism*. His current research focuses on the political and economic consequences of globalization within nations and regions.

**Olga Nazario** (Zaza del Medio, Las Villas, Cuba, 1950) is a political analyst. Her family, like many others, has suffered persecution, exile, political imprisonment, and the firing squad for their opposition to all dictatorships in Cuba. She graduated from the University of Miami with a degree in international affairs.

**Ronalth Ochaeta** is an attorney and diplomat from Guatemala. He studied international law at the University of Notre Dame. He was co-founder and executive director of the Human Rights Office of the

Archdiocese of Guatemala, and institutional director of the Historical Memory Recovery Project.

**Enrique Patterson** (Holguín, Cuba, 1950). An essayist and journalist, he is a human rights activist and also one of the co-founders of the Cuban Social-Democratic Current. He taught the history of the philosophy at the University of Havana. Currently, he is president of the Institute of Cuban Studies. He lives in Miami.

**Pedro Pérez Castro** (Havana, 1936) has lived in Caracas, Venezuela since 1980. He has extensive experience as a trade union leader and a social activist. As a young man, he opposed Batista and then Castro. He served ten years in prison for confronting the current regime as a leader of the *Movimiento de Recuperación Revolucionaria.* He continues the struggle for Cuba and its workers.

**Marifeli Pérez-Stable** (Havana, 1949) is a professor of sociology at Florida International University. She is the author of *The Cuban Revolution: Origins, Course, and Legacy* (Oxford University Press, 1993 and 1999; Spanish version by Editorial Colibrí, Madrid), and has published opinion articles in *El País, The Miami Herald, El Nuevo Herald, Excelsior, Clarín,* and *Encuentro en la Red.* She served as president of the Institute of Cuban Studies from 1994 to 1998.

**Patricia Tappatá de Valdez** is a human rights activist. She was the executive director of the Truth Commission of El Salvador, and the coordinator of human rights services of the Catholic church in Peru. In Argentina, she directs Open Memory and is a member of the board of directors of the Center of Legal and Social Studies.

**José Miguel Vivanco** studied law at the University of Chile and obtained his master's in law (LL.M.) at Harvard University. He worked as an attorney for the Inter-American Commission for Human Rights between 1986 and 1989. In 1990, he founded CEJIL (Center for Justice and International Law), which he directed until 1994. Since then he has been executive director of the Americas Division of Human Rights Watch. He has also been an associate professor of law at the universities of Georgetown and John Hopkins.

**Cristina Warren** directs FOCAL's (Canadian Foundation for the Americas) Research Forum on Cuba. This program seeks to explore the short- and long-term challenges the island has to face. (For more information: www.cubasource.org).

# Select Bibliography

## Cuba

Americas Watch. *Dangerous Dialogue: Attacks on Freedom of Expression in Miami's Cuban Exile Community.* 1992.

*The Homeland Belongs to Us All.* www.fiu.edu/~fcf/zhomelandbelongstousall.html. 27 June 1997.

Human Rights Watch. *Cuba's Repressive Machinery: Human Rights Forty Years After the Revolution.* New York: Human Rights Watch, 1999.

________. *Dangerous Dialogue Revisited: Threats to Freedom of Expression in Miami's Cuban Exile Community.* 1994.

Inter-American Commission on Human Rights. *Annual Report.* Washington: Secretary General of the Organization of American States. 1984-2001.

________. *Seventh Report on the Situation of Human Rights in Cuba.* 4 October 1983.

________. *Sixth Report on the Situation of Political Prisoners in Cuba.* 14 December 1979.

________. *Fifth Report of the IACHR on the Situation of Human Rights in Cuba.* 1 June 1976.

________. *Second Report on the Situation of Political Prisoners and their Family Members in Cuba.* 7 May 1970.

________. *Report on the Situation of Human Rights in Cuba.* 27 April 1967.

________. *Report on the Situation of Political Prisoners and their Families in Cuba.* 17 May 1963.

________. *Report on the Situation of Human Rights in Cuba.* 1 May 1962.

Payá Sardiñas, Oswaldo. *Speech Delivered by Mr. Oswaldo Payá Upon Accepting the Sakharov Prize for Freedom of Thought.* www.cartadecuba.org/ oswaldo_ paya's_speech.htm, 17 December 2002.

"El presidio político en Cuba." *Revista Encuentro de la cultura cubana.* 20 (Spring 2001): 156-240.

*El presidio político en Cuba comunista: Testimonio.* Caracas: ICOSOV Ediciones, 1982.

Proyecto Pensamiento Cubano. www.filosofia.cu/revistas. (With links to the following journals: *Revista Cubana de Ciencias Sociales, Debates Americanos, Contracorriente, Temas, Casa de las Américas,* and *Cuba Socialista*).

Reflection Roundtable of the Moderate Opposition of Cuba. *A Charter of Fundamental Human Rights and Duties of Cubans.* www.cubanuestra.nu/web/article. asp?artID=8d. 20 August 2002.

*Revista Vitral.* www.vitral.org.

Task Force on Memory, Truth, and Justice. memoria.fiu.edu.

United Nations Commission on Human Rights. *Report on the Situation of Human Rights in Cuba, submitted by the Special Rapporteur, in accordance with Commission resolution 1997/62.* 30 January 1998.

________. *Report on the Situation of Human Rights in Cuba, submitted by the Special Rapporteur, in accordance with Commission resolution 1996/69 and Economic and Social Council decision 1996/275.* 22 January 1997.

________. *Report on the Situation of Human Rights in Cuba, prepared by the Special Rapporteur, in accordance with Commission resolution 1995/66.* 7 February 1996.

________. *Report on the Situation of Human Rights in Cuba, prepared by the Special Rapporteur, in accordance with Commission resolution 1994/71.* 11 January 1995.

________. *Report on the Situation of Human Rights in Cuba, prepared by the Special Rapporteur, in accordance with Commission resolution 1993/63.* 24 January 1994.

________. *Report on the Situation of Human Rights in Cuba, prepared by the Special Rapporteur, in accordance with Commission resolution 1992/61.* 4 February 1993.

*The Varela Project.* www.puenteinfocubamiami.org/varela_project_003.htm.

**Other Countries**

Archdiocese of Guatemala, Human Rights Office. *Guatemala: Never Again!/REMHI, Recovery of Historical Memory Project.* Maryknoll, NY: Orbis Books, 1999.

Argentine National Commission on the Disappeared. *Nunca Más: The Report of the Argentine National Commission on the Disappeared.* New York: Farrar, Straus, Giroux, 1986.

Chilean National Commission on Truth and Reconciliation. *Report of the Chilean National Commission on Truth and Reconciliation.* Translated by Phillip E. Berryman. Notre Dame: Notre Dame University Press, 1993.

Commission for Historical Clarification. *Guatemala: Memory of Silence.* hrdata.aaas.org/ceh, 1999.

Commission on the Truth for El Salvador. *From Madness to Hope: The 12-year War in El Salvador.* New York: United Nations, 1993.

Cortes Generales (Spain). *Diario de sesiones del Congreso de los Diputados.* Año 2002, VII Legislatura, Número 625, Sesión número 19. 20 November 2002. Parliamentary debate on the civil war and *franquismo.*

Servicio Paz y Justicia. *Uruguay Nunca Más: Human Rights Violations, 1972-1985.* Translated by Elizabeth Hampsten. Philadelphia: Temple University Press, 1992.

Truth and Reconciliation Commission of South Africa. *Truth and*

*Reconciliation Commission of South Africa Report.* Five volumes. New York: Macmillan Reference, 1998.